The last years of BR steam in Wessex: Southern Region

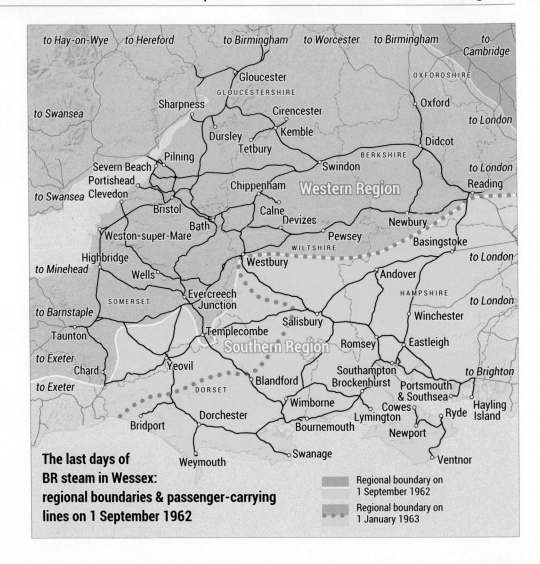

The last days of BR steam in Wessex: regional boundaries & passenger-carrying lines on 1 September 1962

The last years of BR steam in Wessex: Southern Region

Philip Horton

SLP

Silver Link Books

First published in 2021

British Library Cataloguing in Publication Data

A catalogue record for this book is available from the British Library.

ISBN 978 1 85794 577 5

Silver Link Books
Mortons Media Group Limited
Media Centre
Morton Way
Horncastle
LN9 6JR
Tel/Fax: 01507 529535

email: sohara@mortons.co.uk
Website: www.nostalgiacollection.com

Printed and bound in the Czech Republic

Contents

Acknowledgements

I would like to thank those who have helped me with my 'Recollections' of 'The Last Years of BR Steam in Wessex: Southern Region'. Many also contributed to my previous publications, including Stephen Edge, who has provided the map, while Ian Bennett has again allowed me to use coloured photographs taken by the late M. E. J. Deane. I must also thank Frank Hornby, John Price, David Mitchell, Neil Carter and the late Terry Gough for allowing me to use some of their photographs. Other photos have come from my own collection, which includes those taken by my late uncle, Denis Horton.

Many of these 'Recollections' are my own, but I have also obtained much valuable information from contemporary issues of *The Railway Magazine*, *Trains Illustrated* and *Modern Railways*. Of the many books consulted, Hugh Longworth's *British Railways Steam Locomotives 1948-1968*, published by OPC in 2005, provided the building and scrapping dates for the various steam engines, while the dates of station closures are from *The Directory of Railway Stations* by R.V. J. Butt (Patrick Stephens Ltd, 1995).

The text has benefited from the early proofreading and editing carried out by my wife Susan. Finally I would like to acknowledge the help and encouragement received from Peter Townsend of Silver Link Books and Will Adams of Keyword.

Philip Horton
Lincolnshire
June 2021

Introduction

In my earlier book, *The Last Years of BR Steam Around Bath* ('Railways & Recollections' No 64, Silver Link Publishing, 2016), I described the elimination of steam by modern traction in and around the city of my birth. Here I have extended the area covered to the whole of 'Wessex', taken as including Somerset, Dorset, Hampshire, Wiltshire, Gloucestershire and Oxfordshire (see the map). These 'Recollections' are described in two books, *The Last Days of Steam in Wessex: Western Region* and *The Last Days of Steam in Wessex: Southern Region*. This book covers the Southern Region and is Silver Link's 'Railways & Recollections' No 111.

The declining use of steam on the five lines operated by British Railways Southern Region (BR(SR)) within Wessex is chronicled in the following chapters. Their important branch lines, engine sheds and, for Eastleigh, the Works, are also covered. The first two chapters describe routes west of Basingstoke: the SR's 'West of England main line' as far as Yeovil, and that to the 'Strong Country' of Southampton and Bournemouth. The latter also covers the inter-regional trains that ran to the North and Midlands via Oxford as far as Reading (West). Chapter 3 takes us on from Bournemouth, Wareham and Weymouth, while Chapters 4 and 5 look at the southern ends of two inter-regional routes. Those from Bristol/Cardiff to Salisbury and Portsmouth, and trains between Henstridge and Broadstone, were once part of the Somerset & Dorset (S&D) line from Bath and Bournemouth, respectively. Services on the northern parts of both

routes were operated by the Western Region (WR) and are described in my 'Western Region' book ('Railways & Recollections' No 110).

The book's contents are also based on my own recollections and photographs, but as recognised in the Acknowledgments I have made use of the notes published in the railway press, while my own photos are ably supported by those of others. Most of these have not been published before. My own 'trainspotting' days got under way in September 1959 when I changed schools. Initially travelling by train, a small group of us would set off for rail centres such as Salisbury or Eastleigh. In 1964 I acquired a Vespa motor scooter, which increased the opportunities for further visits to these and other rail centres and lineside locations.

Background

After nationalisation the boundary between the Western and Southern Regions changed several times. Between 1958 and 1962 the boundary closely corresponded with that of the former Southern Railway and Great Western Railway (GWR). The trains still largely comprised the engines and stock of the two private companies despite the introduction of BR 'Standard' classes. Radical changes to this boundary occurred at the end of 1962 when the WR took over all SR territory west of Wilton, including the engine shed at Yeovil. The 1958/1962 boundary is shown on the map, together with the area taken over by the WR. This area continued to see the use

of SR engines until the end of steam. I have therefore included it in this book, despite it being operated by the WR from 1963.

In 1955 the 'Railway Modernisation Plan' made significant money available for the first time to update the country's rail network, and was soon being implemented. While other Regions started to replace their fleet of steam engines with diesel power, the SR sought to extend the third-rail electrification it had inherited from the Southern Railway. The first scheme, to the Kent Coast, approved in 1956, was completed in two phases in June 1959 and June 1962. Electrification to

Bournemouth came next, and its implementation in July 1967 saw the end of steam working in southern England. The electrification of the main line from Waterloo to Exeter was also envisaged in the Modernisation Plan, but the transfer of its western end to the WR resulted in dieselisation instead. Steam was virtually eliminated from its western end in September 1964.

The SR's enthusiasm for electrification meant that in 1960 its stock of steam engines still included many of pre-Grouping vintage. These included ex-LSWR Class 'M7' 0-4-4 tank engines and Class '700' 0-6-0s of 1897, together with Class 'T9' 4-4-0s of

1899, the 'Greyhounds'. Post-Grouping engines included 'King Arthur' and 'Lord Nelson' Class 4-6-0s and 'Schools' Class 4-4-0s for passenger work, and Class 'S15' 4-6-0s and Classes 'N' and 'U' 2-6-0s for mixed traffic. The SR had also inherited a stud of modern express passenger engines; these were the 30 'Merchant Navy' Class 'Pacifics' of 1941, followed in 1945 by 110 'West Country' and 30 'Battle of Britain' Class 'Light Pacifics' designed by the Southern Railway's last CME, O.V. S. Bulleid.

Despite this, the idea of replacing steam with diesels was not a new one. Three experimental 1-Co-Co-1 diesel electrics were built for the Southern Railway to Bulleid's design with English Electric engines, two of 1,750hp and one of 2,000hp. They were delivered after nationalisation in 1951, becoming BR Nos 10201 to 10203. The SR also inherited three 0-6-0 diesel shunters (Nos 15201 to 15203) introduced in 1937, again to Bulleid's design with English Electric engines. Twenty-six very similar shunters were built at Ashford from 1949 (Nos 15211 to 15236). The similar BR 0-6-0 shunters (numbered from 13000/D3000 (later Class 08)) followed in 1953. After some test running on the SR's main lines, BR concentrated its few main-line

diesels on the London Midland Region, so that their performance could be compared. After this no more main-line diesels were built for the SR until 1960.

Meanwhile new 'Standard' classes of steam engine started to appear. The engines involved were the Class 5 4-6-0s and Class 4 4-6-0s and Class 4 2-6-0s, together with Class 3 2-6-2 and LMS-designed Ivatt Class 2 2-6-2 tanks. The larger Standard Class 4 2-6-4 tanks also appeared in Wessex in 1962 after being displaced by electrification/dieselisation elsewhere. In addition, all 30 'Merchant Navy' and 60 'Light Pacifics' were rebuilt from 1956 and 1957 respectively to become extremely successful steam locomotives. Examples of these classes were to survive until the end of SR steam in July 1967.

The Type 3 Bo-Bo diesel-electrics (BR Class 33) that started to appear on the SR from 1960 were built to supplement steam, prior to the completion of the Kent coast electrification schemes; they did not appear in Wessex until this work was completed. Electro-diesel locomotives (Class 73) appeared at the same time. It was not until 1966 that six Brush Type 4 Co-Co diesel-electrics (Class 47) were loaned to the Region, again as an interim

measure, prior to completion of the Bournemouth electrification.

Instead of conventional diesel multiple units (DMUs), the SR opted for diesel-electric multiple units (DEMUs). The first to be introduced, in 1957, were the express six-car 'Hastings' units for the line from Cannon Street to Hastings (Classes 201 to 203). In the same year two-car 'Hampshire' units (Class 205), soon strengthened with a third coach, were built at Eastleigh Works for local services in Wessex, particularly in Hampshire and Berkshire.

In the event, despite the introduction of the 'Standard' steam engines together with the DEMUs, the last of the pre-Grouping 'M7s' were not withdrawn until May 1964. Pre-grouping coaches survived on the Isle of Wight until the end of 1966, along with the island's Class 02 0-4-4 tanks. Unlike the WR, the demise of steam on the SR was not greatly helped by the line closures that followed publication of the Beeching Report. Exceptions were the steam-worked lines through Wimborne to Salisbury and Brockenhurst, and the S&D line from Bath (Green Park). As it turned out, dieselised services, including those to Swanage, were soon to close too!

The SR's West of England main line from Waterloo to Exeter crosses my 'Wessex' boundary at Basingstoke. To the east of the station is the junction for the Reading line, while a few miles to the west is Worting Junction, where trains head south towards Winchester (as described in Chapter 2). Several commuter services ran to Waterloo each morning, some of which remained steam-hauled until July 1967.

Basingstoke shed (70D): closed 9 July 1967

I first visited Basingstoke shed on Sunday 25 November 1962. The three-road shed was situated to the north of the main line and west of the station, and included a covered coaling stage and turntable. The 17 steam engines I noted comprised four 'West Country' 'Pacifics', two rebuilt and two in original condition, together with one of Bulleid's Class 'Q1' 0-6-0s, No 33039. Four of the engines present, ex-LSWR Class '700' 0-6-0 No 30368, built in 1897, ex-Southern Railway Class 'V' 'Schools' 4-4-0s Nos 30925 *Cheltenham*, 30926 *Repton* and 30934 *St. Lawrence,* were among the many steam engines withdrawn by the SR at the end of the year. Ex-Southern Railway Class 'S15' 4-6-0 No

30840 and Class 'U' 2-6-0s Nos 31618 and 31806 were also present. Remarkably, four of these were subsequently preserved. *Cheltenham* became part of the National Collection, while *Repton* initially went to the USA but is now at the North Yorks Moors Railway. The two 2-6-0s were withdrawn in January 1964 and went to Barry scrapyard; No 31618 was the second engine to leave there in January 1969 for the Bluebell Railway, while No 31806 left Barry in October 1976 and is now at the Swanage Railway. The three BR 'Standard' engines were 4-6-0s, one Class 5 and two Class 4s.

This sequence of photos taken at Basingstoke shed illustrates how SR steam was modernised between 1955 and 1967. Here on 14 May 1955 all the engines are of pre-nationalisation classes. From left to right, they are Class 'N15' 'King Arthur' 4-6-0 No 30784 *Sir Nerovens*, ex-LSWR Class 'G6' 0-6-0 tank No 30258, an ex-LBSCR Class 'L' 4-6-4 tank, as rebuilt by Maunsell in 1934. Class 'N15X' 4-6-0 No 32331 *Beattie*. The engines were withdrawn in October 1959, July 1961 and July 1957 respectively. *Frank Hornby*

When the WR shed, a sub-shed of Reading, closed in November 1950, its engines were serviced at the SR one. Present on 25 November was ex-GWR 'Grange' 4-6-0 No 6858 *Woolston Grange*. As a portent for the future, two Type 3 diesel-electrics (later Class 33) and two diesel shunters (later Class 08) were also present.

I did not visit Basingstoke shed again until 22 April 1967 when just three BR 'Standard' engines were present, as pictured. These included Class 4 4-6-0 No 75077, a long-time Basingstoke engine that I had spotted there back in 1962.

Above: Also on Basingstoke shed on 22 April 1967 was Class 4 2-6-4 tank No 80152. In the early 1960s this had been a Brighton engine. *Author*

Above: Engines of Victorian vintage could still be seen at Basingstoke shed into 1962. An example was ex-LSWR Class '700' 0-6-0 No 30368, built by Dubs & Co of Glasgow in 1897 and withdrawn in December 1962. Behind is Class 'U' 'Mogul' No 31636. which was withdrawn in June 1963. *Neil Carter*

Right: In contrast, on 22 April 1967 just three BR 'Standard' engines, each of a different class, were on Basingstoke shed, and all lasted until the end of SR steam in July 1967. Seen here is Class 4 4-6-0 No 75077, one of the class fitted with a double chimney and one of the larger Standard BR1B tenders. *Author*

Below: The third engine on Basingstoke shed on that day was Class 5 4-6-0 No 73085. *Author*

Andover Junction

Above: Until September 1964 Andover Junction saw through expresses from Waterloo to Exeter (Central), North Devon and Cornwall, mostly hauled by Bulleid 'Pacifics'. On Sundays the 9.30am train from Waterloo ran only as far as Salisbury. Rebuilt 'Battle of Britain' 'Pacific' No 34056 *Croydon* leaves Andover Junction with the train on Sunday 30 August 1964. The engine was withdrawn in May 1967. *Author*

Above right: Also at Andover Junction on 30 August 1964 was Standard Class 4 2-6-0 No 76066. It is seen heading a train of empty hopper wagons tender-first. The eventual destination of the wagons will be Meldon Quarry near Okehampton in Devon, where the SR obtained its railway ballast. The engine, which is also paired with one of the larger Standard BR1B tenders, lasted until the end of SR steam in July 1967. *Author*

Salisbury in 1964

Right: Merchant Navy' 4-6-2 No. 35026 'Pacific' *Lamport & Holt Line* approaches Salisbury with the 9.00am express from Waterloo to Plymouth and Barnstaple Junction on Friday 4 September 1964. These services were withdrawn from Monday 7 September when almost all West Country trains from Waterloo terminated at Exeter (St. David's). These were hauled by BR(WR) 'Warship' diesel-hydraulics. No. 35026 was withdrawn in March 1967. *John Price*

Salisbury

My earliest recollection of SR main-line steam was at Salisbury in the summer of 1960, when a friend and I spent a day on the platforms there. Sadly my list of numbers disappeared long ago, but I do remember the arrival of the down 'Atlantic Coast Express' and being amazed by its many destinations listed by the station announcer. Other recollections include the arrival of a 'King Arthur' 4-6-0 on a stopping train from Exeter (Central), and of an 'M7' acting as station pilot. Meanwhile SR steam engines were being exchanged for WR examples on trains between Portsmouth and Bristol/Cardiff (see Part 4). The station was not completely diesel-free as three-car 'Hampshire' units (later Class 205) were operating the regular service to Portsmouth & Southsea from the station's eastern bay platform. Finally as our train back to Bath diverged from the SR main line at Wilton, we spotted a 'Schools' Class 4-4-0 approaching Salisbury with a train, probably from Yeovil (Town). Several of the class had recently been posted to the SR's South Western Division following completion of part of the Kent Coast electrification, and dieselisation of trains between Charing Cross and Hastings.

72B **Salisbury shed (72B, later 70E): closed July 1967**

Salisbury was a spacious ten-road shed, situated to the south of the main line west of the station. The turntable was just behind the depot buildings, the line to it passing between them and the coaling plant. To my regret my only visit was on 17 September 1966 when, with many other enthusiasts, we watched the two 'Standard' Class 4 2-6-4 tanks,

Nos 80152 and 80015, being turned and watered. These had taken the 'Flying Scotsman Goes South' special from Eastleigh to Salisbury (see Part 2 and 4). A visit in the summer of 1962 would have revealed a similar mix of engines to Basingstoke but in greater numbers. In addition to Bulleid 'Light Pacifics' the shed was also home to several 'Merchant Navy' engines. Since the ex-GWR shed closed in November 1950 I would also have seen a selection of WR engines.

After July 1967 some 90 SR steam engines were stored there before their dispatch to South Wales scrapyards. These, I discovered later, had included the only Bulleid 'Pacific' I never saw, unrebuilt 'West Country' No 34091 Weymouth. Many of the engines went to Barry scrapyard and were subsequently preserved, but No 34091 was not one of them.

In the first picture unrebuilt 'West Country' 'Pacific' No 34106 Lydford approaches Salisbury with an express from the West Country to London Waterloo on Friday 4 September 1964. Soon afterwards the engine leaves Salisbury with its train for Waterloo, as seen in the second view. In the foreground is the bay platform used by 'Hampshire' DEMUs (later Class 205) on the regular-interval service to Portsmouth & Southsea. John Price

Left: Feltham shed's Class S15 4-6-0 No. 30834 arrives at Salisbury with the 3.20am express freight from Brighton to Salisbury West Yard and Fisherton (*top left*). The train is seen again heading away from Salisbury station on 4 September 1964 (*bottom left*). By then most of these engines were replaced by Caprotti valve gear fitted Standard Class 5 4-6-0s from BR's North Eastern Region at both Feltham and Exmouth Junction sheds. No 30834 was withdrawn in November 1964. while the last active member of its class, No 30837, was not withdrawn until September 1965. *John Price*

Above: Ivatt Class 2 2-6-2T No 41300 runs through Salisbury station on that same September day, as a Standard Class 4 4-6-0 takes water in the platform road. The single white disc on No 41300's smokebox indicates that it may have recently worked an MOD goods train from the Bulford branch. *John Price*

Coal is shovelled forward in the tender as rebuilt 'Battle of Britain' 'Pacific' No 34087 *14 Squadron* waits at Salisbury with the 11.15am from Waterloo to Bude and Padstow. The date is Saturday 5 September 1964, the last day of through services from Waterloo to the West Country. *Author*

Salisbury in 1965

Steam was virtually eliminated from passenger duties west of Salisbury from Monday 7 September 1964. Despite this, one train, the 9.20am Sundays-only stopping train from Salisbury to Exeter (Central), was scheduled for steam haulage during the summer of 1965. Here the fireman of rebuilt 'Battle of Britain' 'Pacific' No 34089 *602 Squadron* climbs down to couple his engine to the train on Sunday 5 September 1965. This was the last occasion that the train was steam-worked, and it ran finally on 26 September. *Author*

A second train that was steam-hauled west of Salisbury during the summer of 1965 was the 8.00am from Waterloo, with through coaches to both Sidmouth and Exmouth; the latter were taken forward from Sidmouth Junction by either a 'Hymek' Type 3 or NB Type 2 diesel-hydraulic. The return working left Sidmouth Junction at 3.05pm, its first stop Salisbury. The train is shown just after arrival at Salisbury on Saturday 31 July 1965 behind Standard Class 5 4-6-0 No 73111, formerly named *King Uther*. This time the fireman is climbing onto the tender to fill its tank with water. The train ran finally on 27 August. *Author*

'A2' Tour at Salisbury in August 1966

The coal-shovellers are busy again on the tender of LNER-designed 'A2' 'Pacific' No 60532 *Blue Peter* at Salisbury on 14 August 1966. The engine is heading the LCGB's 'A2 Commemorative Railtour' from and to Waterloo via Exeter (Central), Exeter (St David's), Taunton, Westbury and Salisbury. The 'Pacific' later disgraced itself by stalling on Honiton Bank and, after arriving very late at Westbury, was declared a failure. 'Britannia' 'Pacific' No 70004 (formerly named *William Shakespeare)* then took the train through to Waterloo. *Blue Peter* was later preserved, while *William Shakespeare* was broken up in April 1968. *Author*

Salisbury shed

Above: One of the original Urie-designed Class 'S15' 4-6-0s, No 30514, built for the LSWR in 1921, is seen at Salisbury shed soon after nationalisation on 19 March 1949, having already received its BR number. Twenty five improved 'S15s' were built by Maunsell from 1927. No 30514 was a Feltham engine for many years and was withdrawn in July 1963. *Frank Hornby*

Above right: On Saturday 17 September 1966 a special train ran from Victoria to Brighton behind preserved ex-LNER 'A3' 'Pacific' No 4472 (BR No 60103) *Flying Scotsman*. The 'Pacific' later hauled the train to Eastleigh, where two 'Standard' Class 4 2-6-4 tanks, Nos 80152 and 80015, took over for the run to Salisbury via Chandler's Ford (see Chapters 2 and 4). Here No 80015 comes off the turntable at Salisbury, while in front of it No 80152 can be seen taking water. *Author*

Templecombe

Below: 'King Arthur', No 30790 *Sir Villiars* of Eastleigh shed, stands in Templecombe station waiting to leave with a stopping train to Exeter (Central) during the summer of 1960. On the left 'Standard' Class 4 2-6-0 No 76011 has arrived on another local train. Oddly neither engine is carrying the distinctive round white discs that indicated the route to be taken by SR trains. No 30790 was one of the 'Scotch Arthurs', built by North British in 1925, and was withdrawn in October 1961. No 76015, then also at Eastleigh shed, lasted until July 1967. *Denis Horton*

'King Arthur' (SR Class 'N15') 4-6-0s were once the principal motive power on expresses from Waterloo to Exeter (Central), but by 1960 the class was rapidly being withdrawn. Another of them, No 30450 *Sir Kay* of Salisbury shed, arrives at Templecombe during the summer of 1960 with a stopping train for Salisbury. The engine was built at Eastleigh in 1925 and was withdrawn in September 1960. One of the class, No 30777 *Sir Lamiel,* is part of the National Collection, based on the heritage Great Central Railway at Loughborough. *M. E. J. Deane collection, courtesy of Ian Bennett*

'Merchant Navy' 'Pacific' No 35019 *French Line CGT* leaves Templecombe with an express from Waterloo to the West Country during the summer of 1961. Note the maroon-liveried coaches on the left, which will later form a train on the ex-S&D line. Trains on the Waterloo main line connected here with those between Bath (Green Park) and Bournemouth (West). Templecombe station closed from 7 March 1966 along with the S&D line. The station reopened in October 1983.
M. E. J. Deane collection, courtesy of Ian Bennett

Rebuilt 'West Country' 'Pacific' No 34048 *Crediton* heads another West Country-bound train at Templecombe during the summer of 1961. It is a Salisbury-based engine, so the train may be the through service from Brighton to Plymouth. *M. E. J. Deane collection, courtesy of Ian Bennett*

Right: On the Thursday before Easter, 15 April 1965, I travelled on the 4.20pm from Bath (Green Park) to Bournemouth (West). At Templecombe it was announced that the train would be held to await the arrival of a relief train, the 4.30pm from Exeter (Central) to Waterloo. I waited at the west end of the platform and was rewarded by the sight of unrebuilt 'Battle of Britain' 'Pacific' No 34057 *Biggin Hill* arriving with the train. As far as I could see, no one left or joined it at Templecombe. I discovered later that the railway author and publisher, the late Michael Harris, was one of the few passengers. *Author*

Yeovil (Junction)

Left: Unrebuilt 'Battle of Britain' 'Pacific' No 34072 *257 Squadron* arrives at Yeovil (Junction) with an express from the West Country to Waterloo during the winter of 1960. No 34072 was withdrawn in October 1964 and went to Barry scrapyard, but was later purchased for preservation and is now active on the Swanage Railway. *M. E. J. Deane collection, courtesy of Ian Bennett*

Another unrebuilt 'Battle of Britain' 'Pacific', No 34086 *219 Squadron*, is seen at Yeovil (Junction) during the winter of 1960. The engine has just arrived at Yeovil with a train from Waterloo and is running round before hauling it, tender-first, to Yeovil (Town). The engine was withdrawn in June 1966. The fine signal gantry controlling the up lines towers above the engine. *M. E. J. Deane collection, courtesy of Ian Bennett*

The SR/WR West of England main line out of Waterloo, 5 September 1964

My first journey from Waterloo to Salisbury was on Saturday 5 September 1964. This was the last Saturday of the summer season and a fateful one for SR's services west of Salisbury. My train left Waterloo at 11.00am behind 'Merchant Navy' 'Pacific' No 35022 *Holland-America Line* with coaches for Ilfracombe and Torrington. It was the last ever 'Atlantic Coast Express'! Being a summer Saturday the train was run in two parts; the first had left Waterloo at 10.35am with the Bude and Padstow coaches. Both trains ran non-stop to Salisbury where water was taken. As my 'ACE' then ran fast to Sidmouth Junction, I left it to catch the 11.15am from Waterloo. This included coaches for Bude and Padstow and arrived behind rebuilt 'Battle of Britain' 'Pacific' No 34087 *145 Squadron*. After taking water this train deposited me at Yeovil (Junction) at 1.33pm. My plan was the catch the 1.40pm push-pull service to Yeovil (Town), but before I could board it the signals came off for an up express and I had time to watch 'Merchant Navy' 'Pacific' No 35009 *Shaw Savill* run through at speed with the last ever up 'ACE' from Padstow and Bude. The train to Yeovil (Town) comprised ex-GWR '64XX' pannier tank No 6430 and two auto-coaches. Since the WR take-over early in 1963 ex-GWR engines had replaced the aged ex-LSWR 'M7' 0-4-4 tanks on these trains. Three Class '54XX' tanks arrived during 1963, but by the summer of 1964 they had been replaced by Class '64XX' engines.

Back at Yeovil (Junction) I watched several expresses, nearly all steam-hauled, pass through on the fast lines. There were few signs of the WR 'Warship' diesel-hydraulics that had officially replaced steam on some of these trains back in August. I planned to return on the 3.48pm to

Yet another unrebuilt 'Battle of Britain' 'Pacific', No 34076 *41 Squadron*, shunts the goods yard at Yeovil (Junction) on 12 February 1964. The engine was withdrawn ten months later. *Author*

Waterloo and, while waiting, watched two trains arrived at Yeovil, again for the last time. The first was a pick-up goods from Exmouth Junction, which arrived behind Class 'U' 2-6-0 No 31791; the second was the two-coach 1.10pm stopping train from Exeter (Central) to Yeovil (Town) headed by unrebuilt 'West Country' 'Pacific' No 34099 *Lynmouth*. My train, the 11.48am from Plymouth, soon arrived behind 'Merchant Navy' 'Pacific' No 35017 *Belgian Marine*. Although I expected this to be my last ever journey from Yeovil (Junction) to Waterloo behind an SR 'Merchant Navy' 'Pacific', it transpired that I was to enjoy one further, final, run.

Yeovil shed (72C, later 83E): closed June 1965

I visited Yeovil shed in August 1963, February 1964 and finally in July 1965. The shed had three roads and was situated on a compact site immediately adjacent to and south of Yeovil (Town) station. Coaling was by means of a steam crane. On 28 August 1963 it contained 14 engines including three unrebuilt 'Battle of Britain' 'Pacifics', three Class 'U' 2-6-0s and three BR 'Standards', Class 5 4-6-0 No 73112 *Lyonnesse*, Class 4 2-6-0 No 76066, and Class 4 2-6-4 tank No 80038. The WR shed at Yeovil (Pen Mill) had closed in January 1959 and five ex-GWR engines were also present: three Class '57XX' pannier tanks and 'Small Prairie' No 4591, all used on the ex-GWR branch line to Taunton, and Class '54XX' pannier tank No 5416 No 5416, one of the ex-GWR engines which replaced the M7 tanks on the Yeovil (town) to (Junction) shuttle service.

In July 1965 just three steam engines remained

A good view of the down-line signals and water tower at Yeovil (Junction) is gained from this shot of Exmouth Junction-based Class 'U' 'Mogul' No 31841 as it arrives with the 9.35am from Exeter (Central) to Salisbury on 12 February 1964. The engine was withdrawn the following month. *Author*

there in store. These were Class '57XX' pannier tanks Nos 9670 and 9754, withdrawn that June, and 'Standard' Class 3 2-6-2 tank No 82035, which had been withdrawn that month.

The SR/WR West of England main line out of Waterloo from 7 September 1964

On the following Monday, 7 September 1964, a totally revised timetable came into force. Semi-fast trains now ran 2-hourly from Waterloo to Exeter (St David's) during the day behind Swindon-

built 'Warship' diesel-hydraulics. 'Stopping' trains were taken over by DMUs, although ten wayside stations were to close together with their goods yards, the latter replaced by a limited number of freight concentration depots. Much of the line was also singled. The new service did not go to plan and there were frequent failures where steam had to fill in. In the summer of 1965 two trains were scheduled for steam-haulage west of Salisbury. One was the Saturdays-only 8.00pm from Waterloo to Sidmouth and Exmouth, steam-hauled as far as Sidmouth (Junction) together with the 3.05pm return. The other was the Sundays-only 9.20am stopping train from Salisbury to Exeter (Central), and 7.36pm return.

At the beginning of 1966 the WR banned all steam west of Salisbury and a privately organised 'Last Steam' special was run from Waterloo to Exeter (Central) on 8 January. Unrebuilt 'West Country' 'Pacific' No 34001 *Exeter* worked the train as far as Salisbury where sister engine, No 34015 *Exmouth*, took over for the run to Exeter.

Despite the ban, a number of specials followed, but as the turntable at Exmouth Junction was no longer available, the trains had to follow a circular route via Exeter (Central), Exeter (St David's) and the WR main line to Westbury, or vice versa. The first of the two I travelled on was the LCGB's 'A2 Commemorative Railtour' behind LNER-designed Class A2 'Pacific' No 60532 *Blue Peter* on 14 August 1966. The train started at Waterloo and ran to Exeter (Central), stalling on Honiton Bank in the process. The engine was eventually taken off the train at Westbury to be replaced by Britannia' 'Pacific' No 70004, once named *William Shakespeare*, which worked the train back to Waterloo via Salisbury. The second, which was the very last run from Exeter (Central) to Waterloo behind a BR-owned steam engine, was the Southern Counties Touring Society's 'West Country Special' on 13 November 1966. This ran from London (Victoria) to Reading (General), with unrebuilt 'West Country' 'Pacific' No 34019 *Bideford* taking over at Westbury. It then hauled the train to Yeovil (Junction) via Exeter (St David's) and Exeter (Central), where the 'West Country' was replaced by 'Merchant Navy' 'Pacific' No 35023 *Holland-Afrika Line* for the run back to Waterloo (see also my 'Railways & Recollections' No 110).

The very last BR steam workings west of Salisbury were a school special on 28 April 1967,

Rebuilt 'Battle of Britain' 'Pacific' No 34087 *14 Squadron* is seen again on Saturday 5 September 1964, the last day of through services from Waterloo to the West Country. It is waiting to depart from Yeovil (Junction) with the 11.15am from Waterloo to Bude and Padstow, while 'Merchant Navy' 'Pacific' No 35009 *Shaw Savill* approaches on the through line with the last up 'Atlantic Coast Express' from Ilfracombe. No 35009 was withdrawn that September and went to Barry scrapyard, from where it was purchased for preservation, but remains unrestored; it is currently reported to be at Riley & Sons yard, Heywood, Greater Manchester. *Author*

which ran from Waterloo to Sherborne behind rebuilt 'Battle of Britain' 'Pacific' No 34052, formerly *Lord Dowding*, and an SR inspection saloon that ran from Weymouth to Yeovil (Junction) and Waterloo on 21 June 1967 behind rebuilt 'West Country' 'Pacific' No 34095 *Brentor*.

A handful of commuter trains between Salisbury and Waterloo remained steam-hauled until July 1967. These included the 6.49am and 7.35am from Salisbury and the 7.18am (7.22am on Saturdays) and 6.51pm from Waterloo. These trains last ran on Saturday 8 July and, when the engine diagrammed

to haul the 7.22am from Waterloo failed, the only replacement was 'Standard' Class 3 2-6-2 tank No 82029. This engine worked the train to Salisbury, then joined the large number of steam engines in store at that time in Salisbury shed.

Another sight never to be repeated at Yeovil (Junction) on Saturday 5 September 1964 is Class 'U' 'Mogul' No 31791 of Exmouth Junction shed arriving tender-first with a pick-up goods from Exeter. The engine survived until June 1966. *Author*

Yeovil (Town) station and shed

Salisbury-based Class 'S15' 4-6-0 No 30831 runs light engine through Yeovil (Town) station in October 1960. The engine was withdrawn in November 1963. The lines into the shed are visible on the extreme right. The station was once operated jointly by the GWR and LSWR, hence the GWR lower-quadrant signals and signal box. It became part of the WR at the beginning of 1963. *M. E. J. Deane collection, courtesy of Ian Bennett*

Left: Ex-GWR auto-fitted tank engines and coaches replaced ex-LSWR 'M7' 0-4-4 tanks on the Yeovil (Town) to Yeovil (Junction) shuttle trains in March 1963, after the lines had become part of the WR. Class '64XX' pannier tank No 6430 stands in the Town station with one of the trains on Saturday 5 September 1964. Steam survived on this service until the end of the year. No 6430 was subsequently preserved and is now at the Severn Valley Railway. Yeovil (Town) station closed in October 1966. *Author*

Right: Yeovil (Town) shed became officially part of BR(WR)'s Newton Abbot Division in September 1963 and was designated 83E. On shed during the winter of 1963 are, from left to right, 'Standard' Class 4 2-6-0 No 76007, Class 'U' 'Mogul' No 31632, and 'Standard' Class 4 4-6-0 No 75003. The engines were withdrawn in July 1967, September 1964 and October 1965 respectively.
M. E. J. Deane collection, courtesy of Ian Bennett

The line to Southampton and Bournemouth left the Salisbury line at Worting Junction, west of Basingstoke. Here a bridge carried the up Bournemouth line over the Salisbury lines, and the four tracks then continued in parallel into Basingstoke station and eastwards towards London. East of the station was the junction for the former GWR line to Reading (West), Oxford and Banbury; this was used by inter-regional trains between Poole, Bournemouth and Portsmouth and the cities of the Midlands and the North. It became part of the SR as far as Southcote Junction outside Reading in 1950.

Basingstoke to Reading (West)

This line was intensively used on summer Saturdays, especially after 1962 when through trains were diverted away from the ex-S&D line. From September 1962 two inter-regional trains ran each weekday and continued to do so until after the end of SR steam. These were the 9.35am from Bournemouth (West) to Liverpool (Lime Street) and Manchester (Piccadilly), the 'Pines Express', followed at 10.50am by the train to York (extended to Newcastle (Central) during the summer). On Thursday 26 August

I followed the progress of both trains from Southampton (Central). That morning the 'Pines Express' arrived there at 10.43am behind unrebuilt 'West Country' 'Pacific' No 34038 *Lynton*, followed at 11.55am by the Newcastle train headed by another unrebuilt 'West Country' 'Pacific', No 34103 *Calstock*. I was hoping for an ex-GWR 4-6-0, but nevertheless boarded the train for Reading (West) where I had planned to wait for the southbound train at 4.03pm. There I photographed ex-SR Class 'N' 'Mogul' No 31816 and Oxford-based ex-GWR 'Grange' 4-6-0 No 6874, formerly named *Haughton Grange*.

When the southbound 'Pines' arrived at 2.45pm, again behind No 34038 *Lynton*, I decided to catch it as I expected the Newcastle train to be hauled by No 34103 *Calstock*. Only afterwards did I discover that only the southbound train was hauled by an ex-GWR 4-6-0! To rectify my error, on 20 October I caught the Poole to York train at Reading (West), this time headed by Standard Class 5 4-6-0 No 73114 *Etarre*. I returned from Oxford behind 'Hall' 4-6-0 No 6952, once named *Kimberley Hall*. When these 4-6-0s were withdrawn at the end of 1965 they were replaced by ex-LMS 'Black 5' 4-6-0s (see my 'Railways & Recollections' No

Basingstoke to Reading (West)

Class 'N' 'Mogul' No 31816 runs light engine through Reading (West) on 26 August 1965, in the process of turning on the triangle of lines there. The twin white discs on the buffer beam indicate that it had earlier arrived from Basingstoke. No 31816 was among the last of its class to be withdrawn, in January 1966. *Author*

In the summer of 1965 two through trains ran daily between the North and Bournemouth (West) via Oxford and Basingstoke. One train came from Newcastle, the other was the 'Pines Express' from Manchester (Piccadilly) and Liverpool (Lime Street). Here the 'Pines' arrives at Reading (West) behind unrebuilt 'West Country' 'Pacific' No 34038 *Lynton* on 26 August 1965. The 'Pacific' will have taken over from a BR(LMR) diesel-electric at Oxford. Additional through trains ran on Saturdays. *Author*

Basingstoke to Bournemouth (West)

Above: The lines from Waterloo to Exeter and Bournemouth diverged at Worting Junction, west of Basingstoke. This was a favourite place for photographs, although I only went there once, on 22 April 1967. After a very long wait the only steam-hauled train, seen here, was headed by a rebuilt 'Bulleid' 'Pacific', which lacked both number and nameplates. In the background is the bridge carrying the up Bournemouth line over those to and from Salisbury. *Author*

Above inset: West of Worting Junction passengers to Bournemouth and Southampton would have been familiar with these hoardings stating: 'You're approaching the STRONG COUNTRY', which included a portrait of an unrebuilt 'Merchant Navy' 'Pacific' on the 'Bournemouth Belle'. The advert referred to the now defunct brewery that produced Strong's Ales and Stouts. This sign is a reproduction, seen adjacent to the heritage Mid-Hants Railway on 26 April 2009. *Author*

110). The train, which travelled via the ex-Great Central line from Banbury to Sheffield (Victoria), last ran on Saturday 3 September 1966 hauled each way between Poole and Banbury by rebuilt 'West Country' 'Pacific' No 34034, formerly *Honiton*. The GCR line closed from the following Monday and the train was rerouted via Birmingham. It remained steam-hauled between Poole and Basingstoke. The 'Pines Express' was diesel-hauled from Crewe to Poole by a Type 4 diesel-electric (later Class 47) from April 1966, although in cases of failures steam sometimes had to deputise.

Eastleigh shed (71A, then 70D): closed 9 July 1967

I first visited Eastleigh's magnificent 15-road shed with a friend in August 1961. Next to the shed building was a massive water tower and coaling stage. We were not bold enough then to enter the shed, but I remember seeing ex-LSWR 'T9' No 30709 dumped next to it; this Exmouth Junction engine had been withdrawn in July. Apart from the preserved ex-LSWR No 120 (BR No 30120), it was the only 'T9' I ever saw. After that I visited the shed quite frequently and was never accosted. Initially it housed a wide range of pre-Grouping engines. The lines on the far side of the shed were then a 'museum' of old engines awaiting breaking up. Visits on a freezing 12 January and a much hotter Easter Saturday, 13 April 1963, after the great cull of SR engines at the end of 1962, were particularly productive. Some of the more interesting classes present are pictured here.

Eastleigh Works (officially closed in 2006 but still used by railway contractors)

Unlike Swindon Works it was only possible to visit Eastleigh Works with a permit, which were only issued to groups. My only visit, on 13 April 1963, was therefore an unofficial one! During it I recorded 32 steam engines, which included many Bulleid 'Pacifics', ex-SR 'Moguls' and various BR 'Standard' engines. The oldest engine there was the only Class 'A1' 0-6-0 'Terrier' tank owned by BR; built in 1876 as LBSCR No 54 *Waddon*, it later became the Southern Railway's, then SR's, Lancing Carriage Works Shunter No DS680, the number

Eastleigh

Many ex-LSWR Class 'M7' 0-4-4 tanks were still active on the SR in the early 1960s. One of them, No 30375, runs light engine on the down centre line at Eastleigh on 11 August 1962. The Eastleigh-based engine was built in 1903 at Nine Elms and withdrawn in September 1962. Although many of its class were push-pull-fitted, No 30375 was not one of them. *Author*

it carried when I 'spotted' it. It had been withdrawn in June 1962 and is now preserved at the Canadian National Railway Museum, Saint-Constant, Quebec. The second oldest was another 'Terrier' tank, LBSCR Class 'AIX' No 35 *Morden*. Also built in 1876, in BR days it became Brighton Works Shunter No DS377 and later No 32635. It carried the name *Brighton Works* and was painted in the LBSCR 'Improved Engine Green' livery (which was basically yellow!). Also present were ex-LSWR Class 'M7' 0-4-4 tank No 30378, Class '700' 0-6-0 No 30695, two 'Schools' Class 4-4-0s, Nos 30917 *Ardingly* and 30937 *Epsom*, and Class 'Z' 0-8-0 tank No 30955.

Left: By 1965 the pre-Grouping engines were long gone, apart from on the Isle of Wight, and trains were worked by BR 'Standard' engines or Bulleid 'Pacifics'. 'Standard' Class 4 2-6-0 No 76007 passes Eastleigh with a parcels train for Southampton Docks on 12 February 1965. The cables althogh appearing to be too low were in fact well above the tracks! *Author*

Below: Unrebuilt 'West Country' 'Pacific' No 34023 *Blackmore Vale* passes slowly through Eastleigh station with a down goods on 2 September 1966. *Blackmore Vale* was withdrawn in July 1967 and subsequently purchased for preservation. It has now been based at the Bluebell Railway for many years. *John Price*

Below: A 'Merchant Navy' 'Pacific' passes Eastleigh with the down 'Bournemouth Belle' on 2 September 1966. By then BR Type 4 diesel-electrics (later Class 47), which had worked the 'Pines Express' to Poole on the Saturday, were used on the train on Sundays. The Fareham lines are in the foreground. *John Price*

Right: On Saturday 17 September 1966 a special train ran from Victoria to Brighton behind preserved ex-LNER 'A3' 'Pacific' No 4472 (BR No 60103) *Flying Scotsman.* The 'Pacific' later hauled the train to Eastleigh where, seen from the crowded platform, it ran to the shed for servicing. Two 'Standard' Class 4 2-6-4 tanks, Nos 80152 and 80015, then took the train to Salisbury via Chandler's Ford (see Chapter 4). *Author*

Eastleigh shed: stored withdrawn engines

Above: In the early 1960s a large number of withdrawn steam engines were stored around Eastleigh shed, in effect creating a fascinating temporary railway museum. On 13 April 1963 these included ex-LSWR 'G6' 0-6-0 tank No DS 683 (formerly BR No 30238). The engine was built at Nine Elms in 1898 and had recently been withdrawn as the SR's service engine at Meldon Quarry, Devon, where it had been replaced by a Class 'USA' 0-6-0 tank. At the time it was the last of its class. None were preserved. *Author*

Above centre: Sixty Class 'O2' 0-4-4 tanks were built for the LSWR at Nine Elms from 1898 for light branch-line work. No 30225 was at Plymouth (Friary) shed for many years, where its duties included both passenger and goods trains between Bere Alston and Callington. When withdrawn in December 1962 No 30225, seen stored at Eastleigh

on 13 April 1963, was the last of its class on the UK mainland, although others survived longer on the Isle of Wight (see Part 4). *Author*

Above right: At the end of 1962 the SR withdrew a large number of its steam engines, many of which I found at Eastleigh during a visit on 12 January 1963. An example was ex-LSWR Class 'G16' No 30494, one of four engines built in 1921 to carry out shunting duties over the newly built 'hump' at Feltham yard. The engine was one of the last two, which were both withdrawn in December 1962. None were preserved. *Author*

Right: Similar in outline to the 'G16' tanks, five Class 'H15' 4-6-2 tanks were built at Eastleigh during 1921, also in connection with the opening of the new marshalling yard at Feltham. The engines were used on transfer goods trains from there to Brent and Willesden and, latterly, on empty stock workings between Clapham Junction and Waterloo. The whole class was withdrawn in November 1962, and No 30517 was still

stored at Eastleigh on 13 April 1963. Again, none were preserved. *Author*

Right: Also at Eastleigh on 12 January 1963 was ex-LBSCR Class 'K' 'Mogul' No 32351, formerly of Three Bridges shed. The engine was one of 17 built at Brighton between 1913 and 1921. All were withdrawn in November and December 1962, and none were preserved. *Author*

Below: Seventy-five Class 'E4' 0-6-2 tanks were originally built for the LBSCR from 1897 for both passenger and goods traffic, and many then carried names. Between 1910 and 1949 the class was rebuilt with new 'Marsh' boilers and extended smokeboxes. No 32503, once named *Buckland*, had just been withdrawn when seen at Eastleigh on 13 April 1963. One of the class, No 32473 (*Birch Grove*) is now preserved on the Bluebell Railway. *Author*

Still active at Eastleigh: 1962-66

Below right: In all, 25 Class 'B4' 0-4-0 tanks were built for the LSWR from 1891. Many worked in Southampton Docks until replaced by Class 'USA' 0-6-0 tanks after the Second World War. Among the last survivors was Bournemouth-based No 30102, seen at Eastleigh on 11 August 1962. The engine was named *Granville* when at Southampton Docks and was withdrawn in September 1963. It is now preserved at Bressingham Steam & Gardens, Norfolk. Sister engine No 30096 (*Normandy*) is at the Bluebell Railway. *Author*

The Class 'T9' 4-4-0s, built from 1899, were the passenger equivalent on the LSWR of the Class '700' goods engines, and were nicknamed 'Greyhounds'. The last examples were active in North Devon and Cornwall until 1961. The Exmouth Junction-based No 30120 (built at Nine Elms in 1899) was the last to be withdrawn, in March 1962. It was then restored to LSWR livery, numbered 120, and worked both service and special trains until July 1963. It is seen at Eastleigh on 11 August 1962. Now part of the National Collection, it has since worked on several heritage railways and is currently at the Swanage Railway. *Author*

Bulleid introduced his 'Austerity' Class 'Q1' 0-6-0s in 1942 to work heavy goods trains on the Southern Railway during the Second World War. Stripped of all unessential equipment, 20 were built at both Brighton and Ashford Works. Feltham (70B)-based No 33006 was at Eastleigh shed on 12 January 1963 and was withdrawn a year later. The first of the class, No 33001, is part of the National Collection and, after many years on the Bluebell Railway, is now at the National Railway Museum at York. *Author*

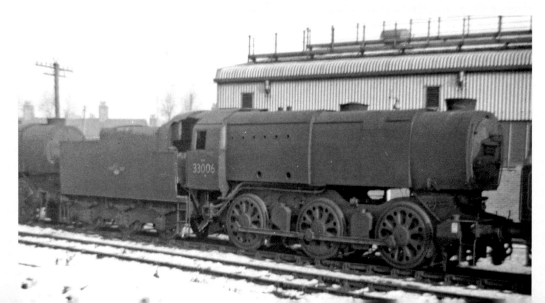

Another legacy from the Second World War were the Class 'USA' 0-6-0 ex-WD engines, which replaced the Class 'B4' tanks at Southampton Docks. Large numbers were built for the American Army (USATC) from 1942, then after the war 13 were purchased by the Southern Railway. In 1961 they were replaced by diesel shunters; six then became SR Departmental engines, while another six worked as shed pilots. All the surviving engines were painted in malachite green livery, an example being No 30073 (built by Vulcan, USA, in 1943) seen at Eastleigh on 2 September 1966. It was withdrawn in January 1967. Four members of the class were subsequently preserved. *John Price*

Southampton (Central)

Above: My last trip behind steam from Waterloo and Weymouth was on 22 March 1967. The electrification third rails are already in place as 'Merchant Navy' 'Pacific' No 35007, formerly *Aberdeen Commonwealth*, passes Southampton (Terminus) station and heads for the tunnel that will bring the 10.30am from Waterloo into the Central station. *Author*

Above right: In the summer of 1960 it was still possible to find one of the older SR engines on express duties. On Saturday 27 August 1960 Nine Elms-based 'King Arthur' 'N15' Class 4-6-0 No 30763 *Sir Bors de Ganis* stands at Southampton (Central) with a relief express from Bournemouth (West) to Waterloo. The engine, another of the 'Scotch Arthurs' built in 1925, was withdrawn in September 1960. *Author*

Right: Looking east at Southampton (Central), 'Merchant Navy' 'Pacific' No 35022 *Holland-America Line* waits to leave on 26 August 1965 with the 9.21am from Weymouth (10.05am from Bournemouth (West)) to Waterloo. Withdrawn in May 1966, No 35022 went to Barry scrapyard and was subsequently preserved; it is yet to be restored *Author*

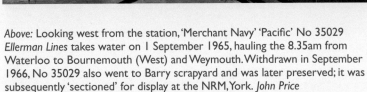

Above: Looking west from the station, 'Merchant Navy' 'Pacific' No 35029 *Ellerman Lines* takes water on 1 September 1965, hauling the 8.35am from Waterloo to Bournemouth (West) and Weymouth. Withdrawn in September 1966, No 35029 also went to Barry scrapyard and was later preserved; it was subsequently 'sectioned' for display at the NRM, York. *John Price*

Above right: Ivatt Class 2 2-6-2 tank No 41319 drifts through Southampton (Central) with a short engineer's train from Redbridge sleeper works to Eastleigh on 26 August 1965. *Author*

Right: Unrebuilt 'West Country' 'Pacific' No 34038 *Lynton* approaches the station with the 9.57am from Bournemouth (West) to Manchester (Piccadilly) and Liverpool (Lime Street), the 'Pines Express', on 26 August 1965. The two white discs above the engine's buffer beam indicate that it will run via Basingstoke and Reading (West) – see above. *Author*

Above: 'Standard' Class 5 4-6-0 No 73043 of Nine Elms shed emerges from the tunnel to the east of Southampton Central station with the 1.30pm from Waterloo to Weymouth on 25 January 1967. The engine lasted until the end of SR steam in July of that year. *Author*

Above right: Eastleigh-based unrebuilt 'West Country' 'Pacific' No 34102 *Lapford* is seen on a van train at Southampton on 25 January 1967. It was to be among the last surviving unrebuilt examples when withdrawn in July 1967. *Author*

Southampton to Bournemouth

Right: West of Southampton on the Bournemouth line, two local stations, Lyndhurst Road and Beaulieu Road, were (and still are) situated within the New Forest. Here rebuilt 'Battle of Britain' 'Pacific' No 34077 *603 Squadron* leans to the curve as it leaves Lyndhurst Road station after calling with the 2.00pm from Eastleigh to Bournemouth (West) on 12 February 1965. One of the engine's nameplates has already disappeared. *Author*

'Merchant Navy' 'Pacific' No 35013 *Blue Funnel* passes Lyndhurst Road with the 4.37pm from Bournemouth (Central) to Waterloo, 'The Bournemouth Belle', on 5 September 1966. *John Price*

Right: Approaching Lyndhurst Road on 12 February 1965, and also leaning to the curve, is 'Standard' Class 4 2-6-4 tank No 80013 with an eastbound van train. The engine had been transferred from Brighton to Bournemouth in June 1964 when services from Brighton to Tunbridge Wells (West) were dieselised. *Author*

Left: Weymouth-based 'Standard' Class 5 4-6-0 No 73020 heads the 1.30pm express from Weymouth to Waterloo past Beaulieu Road on 5 September 1966. *John Price*

The Lymington branch

Between 1960 and 1967 I made several visits to both station and lineside locations between Basingstoke and Bournemouth (Central) as pictured here. One station of particular interest was Brockenhurst, situated about halfway between Southampton and Bournemouth; here trains ran to both Lymington and Bournemouth (West) via Wimborne. The latter are described in Chapter 3. The attraction of the Lymington Pier branch was that, until April 1964, it was push-pull-worked by Class 'M7' 0-4-4 tanks. On 14 April 1963 I travelled on the branch behind 'M7' No 30379, but sadly the weather was appalling. I visited again on a sunny 6 March 1964 when I found 'M7' No 30052 waiting to push the 1.52pm to Lymington Pier, then back. After the 'M7s' were withdrawn that May they were replaced by 'Standard' Class 4 2-6-4 tanks, which had to run round their trains at each end of their journey. The last steam-hauled train ran on 29 March 1967 behind 2-6-4 tank No 80146. The electric third rail was then energised and EMUs took over the service.

Brockenhurst and the Lymington branch

Left: Brockenhurst station, west of Beaulieu Road, was the junction for the lines to Bournemouth (West) via Wimborne and to Lymington. Until 1963 both services were worked by push-pull trains, powered by ex-LSWR 'M7' 0-4-4 tanks. One of these, No 30480, is seen leaving Lymington (Pier) with a train for

Brockenhurst in the summer of 1962. The engine was among the last six to be withdrawn, in May 1964. *M. E. J. Deane collection, courtesy of Ian Bennett*
Above: The proximity of the trains at Lymington (Pier) station (seen to the left) to the Isle of Wight ferry is apparent here and shows the slipway for the Yarmouth ferry during the summer of 1962. *M. E. J. Deane collection, courtesy of Ian Bennett*

Above: 'M7s' continued to power trains to Lymington until May 1964. Here No 30052, another of the last six engines to have survived to that date, is seen at Lymington (Pier) with the 2.16pm to Brockenhurst on 6 March 1964. The Lymington and Swanage branches (see page 52) were the last to see steam-worked push-pull trains on the SR. *Author*

Above right: After the 'M7s' were withdrawn, trains to Lymington (Pier) remained steam-hauled by 'Standard' Class 4 2-6-4 tanks. As these were not push-pull fitted, they had to run round their trains at both Lymington and Brockenhurst. Here No 80085 is shown doing that at Lymington (Pier) on 5 September 1966, at which time it was the last steam-worked branch line. *John Price*

Right and page 44: In the first picture No 80085 heads its train alongside the Lymington River, then arrives at Lymington (Town) station with its train from Lymington (Pier) on 5 September 1966. Note the over-line canopy at the station and the small engine shed – both have since been demolished. The last steam-hauled train ran on 29 March 1967 behind 'Standard' Class 4 2-6-4 tank No 80146. The electric third rail was then energised and EMUs took over the service. *John Price*

Bournemouth (Central)

Left: Among my first ever railway photographs, taken at Bournemouth (Central) on 10 April 1960, is of the last-built 'Merchant Navy' 'Pacific', No 35030 *Elder Dempster Lines*. The engine is seen standing at the up platform, under an array of signals, with an express for Waterloo. No 35030 was built in April 1949 and withdrawn in July 1967. *Author*

Below left: Until 1963 Class 'M7' 0-4-4 tanks were used as station pilots at Bournemouth (Central). During this period one of the class is seen hauling the Bournemouth (West) portion of an express for Waterloo out of the station. The 'M7' will then await the arrival of the train engine with the coaches from Weymouth and will then shunt its carriages onto the rear of the Weymouth train. *Denis Horton*

Below :'Standard' Class 4 2-6-0 No 76025 approaches Bournemouth (Central) with the coaches and restaurant car of a Bournemouth (West) to Waterloo train on 2 September 1965. At the Central station these will be added to coaches from Weymouth, which will shortly arrive behind the train engine. The complete train will then leave for Waterloo. No 76025 is carrying the lamp code for the S&D line out of Bournemouth (West), and the engine will presumably return there to work a train to Bath (Green Park). After the closure of Bournemouth (West) from the following Monday, 6 September, S&D line trains terminated at Central station until the service was withdrawn in March 1966 (see Chapter 5). *John Price*

Eastleigh-based 'Standard' Class 4 4-6-0 No 75074 stands in the bay platform at Bournemouth (Central) on 22 March 1967. In the background 'Merchant Navy' 'Pacific' No 35007 *Aberdeen Commonwealth* takes water while working the 5.30pm from Weymouth to Waterloo. Although Bournemouth (West) station had closed from 6 September, additional coaches and a restaurant car were still added to the train at the Central station. Both engines lasted until the end of SR steam in July 1967. *Author*

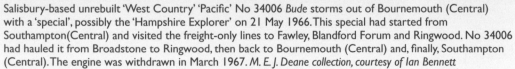

Salisbury-based unrebuilt 'West Country' 'Pacific' No 34006 *Bude* storms out of Bournemouth (Central) with a 'special', possibly the 'Hampshire Explorer' on 21 May 1966. This special had started from Southampton (Central) and visited the freight-only lines to Fawley, Blandford Forum and Ringwood. No 34006 had hauled it from Broadstone to Ringwood, then back to Bournemouth (Central) and, finally, Southampton (Central). The engine was withdrawn in March 1967. *M. E. J. Deane collection, courtesy of Ian Bennett*

Bournemouth shed (71B, then 70F)

One of the attractions of Bournemouth (Central) station was that the yard of its shed was visible from the end of the long down platform. Its motive power changed significantly between April 1960 and 1966, as illustrated here. Prior to the cull of older engines at the end of 1962 it would have included both 'King Arthur' and 'Lord Nelson' Class 4-6-0s. I had arrived there from Pokesdown behind No 30856 *Lord St.Vincent* during Easter 1960. At the time it was also home to ex-LSWR 'T9' 4-4-0s and '700' 0-6-0s. Its dozen or so 'M7' tanks were used on the Lymington branch, from Bournemouth (West) to Brockenhurst via Wimborne, and on the Swanage branch; some of these lasted until May 1964. Ex-GWR 4-6-0s also worked into Bournemouth, initially from Birkenhead (Woodside) and latterly from Oxford on the through train from Newcastle/York. Through this period it also housed a fleet of Bulleid 'Pacifics' and 'Standard' engines, which it retained until July 1967.

Bournemouth shed

Above: By May 1966 Bournemouth shed hosted only BR 'Standard' and Bulleid 'Pacific' engines. From left to right are 'Standard' Class 4 2-6-4 tank No 80152, Class 4 2-6-0 No 76008 and rebuilt 'West Country' 'Pacific' No 34047 *Callington*. The engines were withdrawn in July, April and June 1967 respectively. *M. E. J. Deane collection, courtesy of Ian Bennett*

Left: This is another of my early photos, taken at Bournemouth on 10 April 1960. The shed yard, which could be seen from the down platform at Bournemouth (Central), contains a variety of motive power. Prominent are a rebuilt 'West Country' 'Pacific', a Class 'Q' 0-6-0 and two 'M7' 0-4-4 tanks, and among them is an ex-GWR 'Hall' 4-6-0, which would have worked in earlier on the daily through train from Birkenhead (Woodside) to Bournemouth (West). *Author*

Left: Rebuilt 'West Country' 'Pacific' No 34013 *Okehampton* was on Bournemouth shed on 2 September 1965. This Salisbury-based engine was among the last steam engines to work trains from Salisbury to Exeter (Central) during the summer of 1965 (see Chapter 1) and from Salisbury to Waterloo until July 1967. *John Price*

Bournemouth (Central) and Bournemouth (West)

Another point of interest at Bournemouth was the handling of the through trains from Waterloo to Weymouth. Apart from the 'Channel Island Boat Express', these all included coaches for Bournemouth (West). At Bournemouth (Central) the train engine would first leave with the Weymouth coaches, usually just three during the winter. A second engine would then take the rest of the train, which included the restaurant car, on to Bournemouth (West). For up trains the Bournemouth (West) coaches would arrive first and would then be drawn back on a line that took them opposite the engine shed. This would release the engine that had brought in the coaches to run to Bournemouth shed. The train engine would

Bournemouth (West)

Left: A variety of motive power was used on the Bournemouth (West) coaches off expresses from Waterloo to Weymouth. Here on 23 April 1963 Class 'Q' 0-6-0 No 30541 has brought these into Bournemouth (West) and is waiting to back out of the station ready for its next duty. The Bournemouth-based engine was withdrawn in November 1964 and went to Barry scrapyard; it is now preserved on the Bluebell Railway. *Author*

then arrive with the coaches from Weymouth. The Bournemouth (West) portion was then propelled onto its rear, after which the train would leave for Waterloo. After Bournemouth (West) station closed in October 1965 its coaches were retained at Central station or hauled to the carriage sidings at Branksome, still used today by EMUs.

Waterloo, Basingstoke, Southampton to Bournemouth (Central) in 1966 and 1967

Diesels began to infiltrate the express workings on the line during 1966. On Sundays from 1 May 1966 Type 4 diesel-electrics (Class 47) worked the 'Bournemouth Belle' as a fill-in turn from the 'Pines Express', which did not run on Sundays. Type 3 diesel-electrics (Class 33) also appeared on Saturday extras, and by October were working some trains using the new four-car '4-TC' push-pull units (later Class 491), which from July 1967 would be pushed from Waterloo by the new '4-REP' EMUs (later Class 430). In November three Type 4 diesel-electrics were loaned to the Region with three more arriving a month later. Despite this, partly due to failures of the Class 47s, steam remained prominent. Most of the through Waterloo to Weymouth trains remained steam-hauled, as was the 'Channel Island Boat Express'. During the same period the SR claimed that its huge marshalling yard at Feltham was now steam-free, although contemporary records show that this was not fully achieved until July 1967!

My last trip from Waterloo to Bournemouth (Central) was on the 10.30am to Weymouth on 22 March 1967. The engine was 'Merchant Navy' 'Pacific' No 35007, formerly *Aberdeen Commonwealth*. I travelled with a truly obsessive enthusiast friend (even more so than me!) from UCL. He had spent so much time at Waterloo that he knew a number

of the enginemen and persuaded ours to go for the 'ton' down the bank between Basingstoke and Winchester. After arrival at Southampton (Central) they assured us that 100mph had been shown on the engine's speedometer. This also agreed with the timings taken by my friend from the train. I have my doubts whether either method was 100% accurate, but the train was certainly shifting! At Bournemouth

Above: Rebuilt 'Battle of Britain' 'Pacific' No 34053 *Sir Keith Park* stands in Bournemouth (West) with an express for Waterloo on 2 September 1965 as Ivatt Class 2 2-6-2T No 41295 approaches with empty coaching stock for a later departure from the station. Bournemouth was closed 'temporarily' from 6 September 1965 but never reopened. No 34053 was withdrawn in October 1965 and went to Barry scrapyard, but was subsequently preserved; after working on several heritage railways it is now at the Spa Valley Railway, Tunbridge Wells. *John Price*

(Central) I remained on the train and, after the Bournemouth coaches were detached, enjoyed a peaceful journey to Weymouth (see Chapter 3). I returned from Weymouth on the 5.30pm to Waterloo headed again by No 35007 to meet up with my friend once more at Bournemouth.

A series of special trains were run to celebrate the end of steam on the SR. Saturday 3 June saw

Above: No 34053 *Sir Keith Park* joins the main line from Weymouth to Bournemouth (Central) at Gas Works Junction signal box with an express for Waterloo on 2 September 1965. No 34053 was withdrawn in October 1965 and went to Barry scrapyard, but was subsequently preserved. It has since worked on a number of heritage railways. *John Price*

privately preserved 'A4' 'Pacific No 4498 *Sir Nigel Gresley* (BR No 60007) run from Waterloo to Bournemouth (Central). It then returned the train to Southampton (Central), where 'West Country' 'Pacific' No 34023, formerly *Blackmore Vale*, took it on to Salisbury via Chandler's Ford. No 4498 then returned the train to Waterloo. Next day the 'Pacific' ran from Waterloo to Weymouth and return. BR ran two specials on Sunday 2 July. The 'BR Farewell to Southern Steam No 1' ran from Waterloo to Weymouth behind 'Merchant Navy' 'Pacific' No 35007, once named *Aberdeen Commonwealth*. It was then double-headed out of Weymouth with 'Merchant Navy' 'Pacific' Nos 35008, once named *Orient Line*, as far as Bournemouth (Central). No 35008 was then taken off and No 35007 returned the train to Waterloo. The 'BR Farewell to Southern Steam No 2' special ran from Waterloo to Bournemouth (Central) and returned behind the now preserved 'Merchant Navy' 'Pacific' No 35028 *Clan Line*.

The final steamed-hauled service train to arrive at Waterloo on Sunday 9 July was the 2.11pm for Weymouth hauled by 'Merchant Navy' 'Pacific' No 35030, once named *Elder Dempster Lines*. The last departure was a boat train special, which left for Southampton Docks at 6.20pm behind rebuilt 'West Country' 'Pacific' No 34037, once named *Clovelly*. Sadly I was busy elsewhere, so missed these last rites.

Part 3: BOURNEMOUTH (Central) and (West) to WEYMOUTH (Quay) including the lines to WIMBORNE, BROCKENHURST and SALISBURY, WAREHAM and the SWANAGE branch, and WEYMOUTH (Town)

The splitting of Waterloo trains into Weymouth and Bournemouth (West) portions at Bournemouth (Central) is described in Part 2. In the summer of 1962 Bournemouth (West) saw departures to a wide range of destinations. The station was situated on a spur to the south of the Weymouth line at Branksome; trains from the east ran into it at Gas Works Junction, those from the west at Branksome Junction. These two lines met north of the station at Bournemouth (West) Junction, thus forming a triangle of lines. The former S&D engine shed at Branksome was in the 'Y' of the two lines; by 1962 this was a sub-shed of Bournemouth, but was still used to service engines.

In 1962 departures from Bournemouth (West) for Waterloo, including the 'Bournemouth Belle', ran via Gas Works Junction, together with through trains to both Birkenhead (Woodside) and Newcastle (Central). Trains to Templecombe and Bath (Green Park), including the 'Pines Express' to Liverpool (Lime Street) and Manchester (Piccadilly), used Branksome Junction, as did three through trains to

Bournemouth (West) to West Moors

By 1964 the 'M7s' had been replaced by non-push-pull-fitted engines on trains from Bournemouth (West) to Brockenhurst via Wimborne. On 6 March 1964 'Standard' Class 4 2-6-0 No 76019 enters Broadstone with the 12.26pm from Bournemouth West. The passenger accommodation still comprised one of the two-coach push-pull sets. At Brockenhurst No 76019 had to run round its train and turn on the turntable there. The service was withdrawn in May 1964. *Author*

Above: Another 'Standard' Class 4 2-6-0 No 76055 arrives at West Moors with the 4.50pm from Bournemouth (West) to Salisbury via Fordingbridge on 6 March 1964. The fireman can be seen receiving the token from the signalman for the single line. This service was also withdrawn in May 1964. *Author*

Wareham and the Swanage branch

Above right: 'Merchant Navy' 'Pacific' No 35008 *Orient Line* heads out of Wareham over the level crossing and past the signal box with the 1.25pm from Weymouth to Waterloo on 4 August 1966. *Author*

Right: Standard Class 4 2-6-0 No 76007 arrives at Wareham with the 3.01pm Bournemouth (Central) to Weymouth on 4 August 1966. The bay platform for Swanage is on the right. *Author*

Bristol (Temple Meads)(see Chapter 5). Trains to Brockenhurst and Salisbury via Wimborne also used the western junction. Many more through trains ran on summer Saturdays, especially via the ex-S&D line, while other summer trains ran via Wimborne to Salisbury and Westbury.

From 10 September 1962 the 'Pines Express' was diverted away from the old S&D route to run via Basingstoke and Oxford (see Chapter 2), and in the summer of 1963 all through trains from the north used this route. After Bournemouth (West) closed from 6 September 1965, the S&D line trains terminated at Central station, while the remaining through trains terminated at Poole.

Lines to Brockenhurst and Salisbury via Wimborne

In 1962 most Brockenhurst trains were push-pull-worked using 'M7' tanks, while 'Standard' Class 4 2-6-0s were used on those to Salisbury. By the end of 1963 the demise of the 'M7s' was imminent. Nevertheless, on 6 March 1964 I travelled from Bath (Green Park) to Broadstone hoping to find one still at work. At Broadstone I caught the 12.26pm from Bournemouth (West) to Brockenhurst, but the train arrived behind 'Standard' Class 4 2-6-0 No 76019, although it was hauling a Maunsell push-pull set. At Brockenhurst the 2-6-0 would have had to run round its train and use the turntable there, before returning to Bournemouth. As described in Part 2, I did find one of Bournemouth's 'M7s' working the Lymington branch.

I returned as far as West Moors behind 'Standard' Class 5 4-6-0 No 73022 on the 4.07pm from Brockenhurst, which turned out to be the school train. At West Moors a single line left the Wimborne to Brockenhurst line for Salisbury. My

Right: The branch lines to Lymington and Swanage were the last to see push-pull trains worked by 'M7' tank engines. Here No 30053 pulls into the Swanage bay platform at Wareham on 25 April 1964 during the last few days of push-pull operation on the branch. After taking water it left again with the 6.28pm to Swanage. All remaining 'M7s' were withdrawn in May. No 30053 was purchased for preservation in the USA but has since returned to the UK and has been running on the Swanage Railway for many years. *Author*

Right: After withdrawal of the last 'M7s' the Swanage branch was worked by Standard Class 4 2-6-4 and Ivatt Class 2 2-6-2 tanks, which had to run round their trains at the end of each journey. Here 'Standard' tank No 80138 takes water while waiting in the bay platform at Wareham with the 3.44pm to Swanage on 4 August 1964. DEMUs replaced steam on the branch in September 1966, but the service was withdrawn in January 1972, despite not being listed in the Beeching Report. *Denis Horton*

train, the 4.50pm from Bournemouth (West), arrived behind another Standard Class 4 2-6-0 No 76055. By the time I reached Salisbury it was nearly dark and I can remember seeing the warning red light on top of the city's cathedral spire as we ran into the station. From Salisbury I caught the 5.00pm from Waterloo to Yeovil (Town) behind rebuilt 'Battle of Britain' 'Pacific' No 34109 *Sir Trafford Leigh-Mallory* and, after a wait of almost an hour at Templecombe, arrived back at Bath (Green Park) at 10.21pm. The services to Brockenhurst and Salisbury were both withdrawn from 5 May.

Wareham to Swanage

The Swanage branch leaves the Weymouth line at Worgret Junction, west of Wareham station. I remember a family day trip to Swanage in 1959 – once on the beach I was soon asking my father if we could go to the station! There I saw my first 'M7' with a train to Wareham. I also 'spotted' a rebuilt 'West Country' 'Pacific' waiting with a through train to Waterloo, while in the goods yard was the station pilot, an ex-LSWR Class '700' 0-6-0. The turntable there was not long enough to turn a Bulleid 'Pacific', so these had to travel the branch line tender-first in one direction.

Again, with the imminent demise of the 'M7s', I travelled to Wareham on 25 April 1964 in the hope of finding one still at work. I was in luck as No 30053 stood in Wareham's bay platform with the 4.57pm to Swanage. Two trains were needed to work the Swanage branch each day, and the other was being worked by Standard Class 3 2-6-2 tank No 82028. Had I planned to catch the 6.28pm from Wareham I would have missed my journey with an 'M7'! These were the final days for the class as all were withdrawn that May. After a spell in the

Ivatt Class 2 2-6-2 tank No 41316 stands in the bay platform at Wareham with the 2.10pm to Swanage on 4 August 1966. *Denis Horton*

USA No 30053 is now back home on the heritage Swanage Railway.

On my next visit on 4 August 1966 the branch's two trains were hauled by Standard Class 4 2-6-4 tank No 80138 and Ivatt tank No 41316. This was to be my last steam-hauled journey on the branch in BR days as 'Hampshire' DEMUs took over the service a month later. Various steam specials visited the branch until the end of SR steam, while Waterloo trains continued to use the branch during the summer until the service was withdrawn from 3 January 1972. The line is now operated by the heritage Swanage Railway.

Dorchester (South)

Dorchester has long had two stations, Dorchester (West) on the former GWR line from Yeovil (Pen Mill) to Weymouth, and Dorchester (South) on the former Southern Railway line from Bournemouth. These two lines to Weymouth met at Dorchester Junction and, by the 1960s, were both controlled by the SR. Dorchester (South) station was an anomaly. When it was opened in 1847 the Southampton & Dorchester Railway hoped to eventually reach Exeter, so the line ended heading due west. In the event the line was extended to Weymouth, so turned sharply south just short of the old terminus station; thereafter all trains had to reverse either into or out of the station. A platform opened on the down line in the 1870s but up trains continued to use the old terminus. A new platform on the up curve was not provided until 1970.

The nameboard at Swanage station is reflected in the window of the Bulleid coach, part of the 2.35pm to Wareham headed by Standard Class 4 2-6-4 tank No 80138 on 4 August 1966. *Author*

Dorchester (South)

The up and down platforms at Dorchester (South) were famously not aligned. Here 'Merchant Navy' 'Pacific' No 35008 *Orient Line* stands in the up platform with the 1.25pm from Weymouth to Waterloo on 4 August 1966. To reach the platform No 35008 has had to pass the junction for it, then reverse into it. The down platform was situated on the sharp curve taken by through trains between Bournemouth and Weymouth (extreme left). An up platform has subsequently been built opposite it and the old station closed. *Author*

Right: 'West Country' 'Pacific' No 34108 *Wincanton* stands at the down platform at Dorchester (South) with the 1.30pm from Waterloo to Weymouth on 22 March 1967. The photo is taken from the 5.30pm from Weymouth to Waterloo, which has reversed into the up platform. *Author*

Bincombe Tunnel

Below: On Saturday 7 August 1965 I spent the day at the lineside near to both the north and south portals of Bincombe Tunnel outside Weymouth. The only ex-GWR engine I saw that day was 'Grange' 4-6-0 No 6838, formerly named *Goodman Grange*, seen heading away downgrade from the north end of the tunnel with the 11.05am from Weymouth to Wolverhampton (Low Level). The engine was withdrawn from Worcester shed (85A) in November 1965. *Author*

Below right: On that August day the Channel Islands boat train was run in two portions. The second train, headed by 'Merchant Navy' 'Pacific' No 35023 *Holland-Afrika Line*, is seen approaching the north end of Bincombe Tunnel. *Author*

Now overlooking the north portal of the tunnel, two 'Standard' Class 5 4-6-0s, Nos 73020 and 73118 (once named *King Leodegrance*), emerge with the 1.30pm from Weymouth to Waterloo. At Dorchester (South) the train will have to reverse into the up platform, but before this No 73020 will have been uncoupled to return light engine to Weymouth. Trains not stopping at Dorchester were banked out of Weymouth, and a refuge siding used by the banking engines can be seen in the left foreground. *Author*

We are now at the Weymouth (south) end of Bincombe Tunnel, also on Saturday 7 August 1965. 'Standard' Class 5 4-6-0 No 73085 (formerly named *Melisande*) passes the site of Upwey Wishing Well Halt (closed in 1957) with the first portion of the Channel Islands boat train; the train is banked in the rear by No 73020, which had returned earlier from Dorchester. Both engines were withdrawn in July 1967. *Author*

'Battle of Britain' 'Pacific' No 34077 *603 Squadron* (but missing its nameplate) climbs the steep bank out of Weymouth with the second portion of the Channel Islands boat train, banked in the rear by 'Merchant Navy' 'Pacific' No 35017 *Belgian Marine*. Is the engine providing the 'Tiger in the Tank' as claimed by the advert of the times for Esso petrol? *Author*

Weymouth and Weymouth (Quay)

An Ivatt Class 2 2-6-2 tank marshals a parcels train in the sidings at Weymouth on 4 August 1966. *Author*

Above: BR 'Standard' Class 4 2-6-0 No 76018 stands in Weymouth station with a train for Bournemouth (Central) on 2 September 1965. In the background a DMU waits in the bay platform forming a service for Bristol (Temple Meads). *John Price*

Above right: My last steam-hauled journey from Waterloo was on 22 March 1967 aboard the 10.30am to Weymouth. The train, headed by 'Merchant Navy' 'Pacific' No 35007 (once named *Aberdeen Commonwealth*) is seen here after arrival at Weymouth. Most of its carriages and restaurant car had been removed at Bournemouth (Central), where the train's length was reduced to just three coaches. *Author*

Right: By March 1967 many steam services on the Bournemouth line had been taken over by main-line diesels. However, most of the through trains to Weymouth remained steam-hauled, together with several local trains. On 22 March rebuilt 'West Country' 'Pacific' No 34025 (formerly named *Whimple*) approaches Weymouth with the 3.01pm stopping train from Bournemouth (Central). *Author*

Weymouth (Quay)

The seaside resort of Weymouth was another popular destination for a weekend visit by my family, so another early memory is of being taken to the town's harbour to see the trains run through the dockside street to Weymouth (Quay). Both goods and passenger traffic were handled, the latter involving the daily Channel Islands boat train from London. Traditionally these trains had run from Paddington via Yeovil (Pen Mill), but in 1960 the service was taken over by the SR and run from Waterloo. In 1934 the GWR built six small Class '1366' 0-6-0 pannier tanks for dockside use, three of which were based at Weymouth. In 1961 one of these would replace a Bulleid 'Pacific' outside Weymouth station and work the train along the tramway to Weymouth (Quay). This involved a railwayman walking in front of the train with a red flag, hoping that no parked cars were fouling the running line. On summer Saturdays the Quay was a busy place as two separate boat trains ran from Waterloo. These tank engines were replaced by BR-built diesel shunters (later Class 03). However, steam did not disappear from the Quay altogether, as I remember seeing an ex-GWR Class '57XX' pannier tank work a van train along it in June 1964. Regular passenger trains to the Quay ceased in 1987 and the tramway, having been 'mothballed' for many years, has now been ripped up.

A feature of Weymouth was the tramway that led to Weymouth Quay and boats to the Channel Islands. The line was used by both the Channel Islands boat trains and goods traffic. For many years trains were worked over it by ex-GWR Class '1366' pannier tanks, three of which were allocated to Weymouth shed. One of these, No 1368, heads a van train, probably carrying bananas, along the Quay towards the main line in August 1960.
M. E. J. Deane collection, courtesy of Ian Bennett

82F

Weymouth shed (82F, then 71G, finally 70G): closed July 1967

The shed was a classic GWR straight shed with four roads, one of which led to a lifting shop. The coaling plant and turntable were to the east of the shed building. At nationalisation it had a complement of 25 ex-GWR engines, including three Class '1366' pannier tanks. In 1962 three of the class were transferred to Wadebridge, where they replaced the Beattie 'well tanks' on china clay traffic. After withdrawal in October 1964, one of them No 1369 was preserved and is now at the South Devon Railway. After the Southern Railway's small shed at Weymouth closed in 1938, the facilities at the GWR shed were shared between the two companies. The shed came under SR control in 1958.

By the spring of 1964 the shed still had an allocation of 29 engines, although apart from visiting 4-6-0s the ex-GWR contribution was just a couple of Class '57XX' pannier tanks. SR engines included some Class 'N' 2-6-0s, but the 'Merchant Navy' and 'Light Pacifics' present were also just visitors. Otherwise Ivatt Class 2 2-6-2 tanks and Standard Class 5 4-6-0s and Class 4 2-6-0s dominated.

Standard ex-GWR '57XX' pannier tanks were also allowed on the line to Weymouth (Quay). Here in the summer of 1959 one of the class heads another van train along the Quay. The notice on the engine's smokebox reads 'Danger Keep 50ft Clear'. The train is preceded by a railwayman whose job it was to ensure that any vehicles were indeed 50 feet clear. Cars parked adjacent to the lines were a continuing problem, especially in summer. Latterly a police escort was also employed. *Denis Horton*

On 3 July 1966 the branch was visited by the LCGB's 'Green Arrow Railtour' from Waterloo. The expected ex-LNER 2-6-2 No 60919 failed at Nine Elms and was replaced by unrebuilt 'West Country' 'Pacific' No 34002 *Salisbury*. The train later arrived at Weymouth behind No 34100 *Appledore* and 'Black 5' No 45493. As scheduled, Ivatt Class 2 2-6-2 No 41298 was used on the line to Weymouth (Quay) and is seen making its way slowly along it among the parked cars.
M. E. J. Deane collection, courtesy of Ian Bennett

Bournemouth (Central) to Weymouth in 1965-67

As pictured on pages 55-57, I spent most of Saturday 7 August 1965 at the lineside on either side of Bincombe Tunnel, situated at the top of the long incline out of Weymouth. On summer Saturdays several Waterloo to Weymouth trains included a restaurant car and did not lose it at Bournemouth (Central). A succession of long expresses therefore passed me, including the two Channel Islands boat trains. The only diesel-worked trains came from the WR and were mainly DMUs.

A year later on Thursday 4 August 1966 I travelled by car to Weymouth with my Uncle Denis (an SR signalman in South London) with the aim of visiting the Swanage branch. At Weymouth we boarded the 1.25pm to Waterloo headed by 'Merchant Navy' 'Pacific' No 35008 *Orient Line*. We left the train at Wareham where, as described above, we travelled to Swanage and back. We returned to Weymouth on the 3.01pm stopping train from Bournemouth (Central) behind Standard Class 4 2-6-0 No 76007. When we stopped at Dorchester (South)'s down platform, I could see rebuilt 'Battle of Britain' 'Pacific' No 34071 *601 Squadron* standing in the up terminus platform with the 3.50pm from Weymouth to Waterloo. It is noteworthy that all the SR engines we saw that day still carried their nameplates.

Despite the arrival of the Type 4 diesel-electrics (Class 47) on the SR at the end of 1966, many of the Waterloo to Weymouth trains remained steam-

hauled, particularly the Channel Islands boat trains. My final journey from Waterloo to Weymouth and back was, as described in Part 2, on 22 March 1967 behind 'Merchant Navy' 'Pacific' No 35007. Like all SR engines at the time it had lost its nameplates and looked generally run-down. At Weymouth I watched the 3.50pm to Waterloo leave behind 'West Country' 'Pacific' No 34034, once named *Honiton*, and sister engine No 34025, once named *Whimple*, arrive with the 3.23pm stopping train from Bournemouth (Central). Finally, before my own departure for Waterloo at 5.30pm, 'Standard' Class 4 2-6-0 No 76008 left with the 4.47pm stopping train to Bournemouth (Central).

As also described in Part 2, a number of steam specials arrived at Weymouth during 1967. These included one headed by privately preserved 'A4' 'Pacific No 4498 *Sir Nigel Gresley* (BR No 60007) on Sunday 4 June, and BR's 'Farewell to Southern Steam No 1' on Sunday 2 July behind 'Merchant Navy' 'Pacific' No 35007. Leaving Weymouth, this was double-headed as far as Bournemouth (Central) by 'Merchant Navy' 'Pacifics' Nos 35007 and 35008, the latter once named *Orient Line*.

The final BR steamed-hauled train to arrive at Waterloo from Weymouth on Sunday 9 July was the 2.11pm, behind 'Merchant Navy' 'Pacific' No 35030, once named *Elder Dempster Lines*.

Ivatt Class 2 2-6-2 tank No 41324 stands between a Standard Class 4 2-6-0 and a Bulleid 'Pacific' at Weymouth shed on the same day. The tender of another Standard Class 4 2-6-0 is seen on the right. *John Price*

Weymouth shed

Rebuilt 'West Country' 'Pacific' No 34093 *Saunton* heads for Weymouth shed after bringing an express into the town's station on 2 September 1965. The position of the white discs indicates that the engine has worked through from Waterloo, possibly on the Channel Islands boat train. *John Price*

For many years several trains a day had run between either Bristol (Temple Meads) or Cardiff (General) to Salisbury, Southampton (Central) and Portsmouth & Southsea. These remained steam-hauled into 1962, after services to Paddington had been dieselised. Although WR diesel-hydraulics took over the trains during 1962, they remained steam-hauled beyond Salisbury for much longer. In the early 1960s one was a through train from Cardiff (General) to Brighton, which detached coaches for Portsmouth & Southsea at Fareham. Two other trains running at that time were from Bournemouth (West) via Southampton (Central) and from Plymouth to Brighton via Okehampton, Exeter (Central), Salisbury and Southampton (Central). The latter also included coaches for Portsmouth & Southsea, detached at Fareham. While the Plymouth train continued to run into the 1970s, the others disappeared after a few years.

I used the trains from Bristol (Temple Meads) or Cardiff (General) when visiting Eastleigh and its shed as described in Part 2. Only later did I extend my journeys to Portsmouth when visiting the Hayling Island branch or to reach the ferry to the Isle of Wight. After passing Cosham my train would have left the main line to Brighton at Cosham Junction to join the electrified line used by the EMUs from both Waterloo and Brighton at Portcreek Junction. These, together with the regular 'Hampshire' DEMUs (later Class 205) forming stopping trains to and from Salisbury, meant that steam-worked services were relatively few. The exceptions were the through trains, for as long as they ran, together with parcels and goods traffic. Their engines were serviced at Fratton shed, although after November 1959 it was only a sub-shed of Eastleigh.

Salisbury to Southampton (Central) and Portsmouth (Harbour)

BR 'Standard' Class 4 4-6-0 No 75074 has arrived at Salisbury with a train from Portsmouth & Southsea to Cardiff (General) on 4 September 1964. The loco will be replaced here by a 'Hymek' diesel-hydraulic, which will take the train on to its destination. *John Price*

The line between Southampton and Salisbury saw flows of traffic between South Wales, Bristol and the South Coast. There was also a daily through train from Brighton to Plymouth, via Exeter (Central). Both services remained steam-hauled to Salisbury, at least into 1965. On Sunday 30 August 1964 'Standard' Class 5 4-6-0 No 73088 *Joyous Gard* brings the 2.15pm from Portsmouth & Southsea to Cardiff (General) through Romsey station. *Author*

Right and below: On Saturday 17 September 1966 a special train ran from Victoria to Brighton behind preserved ex-LNER 'A3' 'Pacific' No 4472 *Flying Scotsman.* The 'Pacific' later hauled the train to Eastleigh (as pictured on page 30), where two 'Standard' Class 4 2-6-4 tanks, Nos 80152 and 80015, took the train on to Salisbury via Chandler's Ford. Here the two 'Standard' tanks are seen during a photo stop at Romsey. As will be noted, the train's passengers were not inhibited from trespassing all over the running lines and climbing one of the signal posts! *Author*

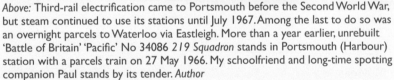

Above: Third-rail electrification came to Portsmouth before the Second World War, but steam continued to use its stations until July 1967. Among the last to do so was an overnight parcels to Waterloo via Eastleigh. More than a year earlier, unrebuilt 'Battle of Britain' 'Pacific' No 34086 *219 Squadron* stands in Portsmouth (Harbour) station with a parcels train on 27 May 1966. My schoolfriend and long-time spotting companion Paul stands by its tender. *Author*

Top right: Fratton shed (70F), outside Portsmouth, lost its own allocation of steam engines in November 1959 when it became a sub-shed of Eastleigh. However, it continued to turn and service them until the end of SR steam in July 1967. Although Class 'A1X' 0-6-0 tank No 32655, seen at Fratton shed on 24 July 1948, was withdrawn in May 1960, others of its class remained in use on the Hayling Island branch until it closed in November 1963. Built at Brighton to Stroudley's design in June 1878 as a Class 'A1', No 32655 was once LBSCR No 55 *Stepney* and has now been preserved on the Bluebell Railway for almost 60 years. Like most of its class it was rebuilt by Marsh between 1911 and 1947, and reclassified 'A1X'. *Frank Hornby*

The Hayling Island branch

At the beginning of 1963 I decided that I must visit the Hayling Island branch, which, because of the severe weight restriction over Langstone Harbour Bridge, was still worked by ex-LBSCR 0-6-0 'Terrier' tanks of Class 'A1X'. Despite it being in the middle of the coldest weather for a generation, I set off for the South Coast from Bath Spa on Saturday 12 January. After a visit to Eastleigh shed (see Chapter 2) I arrived at Havant at 2.13pm and waited by the bay platform used by the island trains. The branch line enjoyed a regular service that became quite intensive on summer Saturdays. A few minutes later a small tank engine appeared bunker-first and completely dwarfed by its two coaches. The engine, Class 'A1X' No 32661, quickly ran round its coaches and just 5 minutes later at 2.20pm we were off to Hayling Island. After crossing the bridge onto the island, the branch runs alongside the seashore. That day the sea was quite a sight as it was completely frozen over and only a few beachcombers wandered disconsolately along the beach.

After arrival at Hayling Island No 32661 ran round its train, stopping halfway along the loop to be coaled by hand from the small coal stage there (as pictured). The engine was built in 1875 as

Havant to Hayling island

Left: Class 'A1X' 0-6-0 tank No 32678 stands in the Hayling Island bay at Havant station during 1963. The engine was built in July 1880 as LBSCR No 78 *Knowle*, and also spent time on the Isle of Wight as No W14 *Bembridge*. It has been preserved on the Kent & East Sussex Railway for many years.
Ray Ruffell, Slip Coach Archive

LBSCR Class 'A1' No 61 *Sutton*, later receiving a Marsh boiler to become Class 'A1X'. It was withdrawn in April 1963 and sadly not preserved. I returned to Havant at 3.10pm and eventually caught the 5.45pm from Portsmouth & Southsea to Cardiff (General) behind a Standard Class 4 2-6-0. The tale of my long wait at Salisbury while the authorities tried to de-ice a WR 'Hymek' diesel-hydraulic is told in my 'Western Region' book ('Railways & Recollections' No 110).

The last Saturday of the Hayling Island branch, 2 November 1963

Services on the Hayling Island branch were withdrawn from Monday 4 November, so on Saturday the 2nd I left Bath Spa at 11.09am and, after changing at Fratton, arrived at Havant at 3.07pm. Although it was cold the sun shone out of a cloudless sky. At Havant I found the summer timetable in operation with two trains running. One stopped at both intermediate stations while the other ran fast between Havant and the Island. After travelling to Hayling Island I returned to North Hayling to watch the trains go by! There I saw three ex-LBSCR 'Terrier' Class 'A1X' tanks, Nos 32650 (built in 1876 as No 50 *Whitechapel*) and 32662 (built in 1875 as No 62 *Martello*). The third engine was No 32670 (built in 1872 as No 70 *Poplar*). In 1901 this was sold to the Kent & East Sussex Railway, becoming that line's No 3, but when BR took over the line in 1947 it was renumbered 32670. All were withdrawn in November 1963 and subsequently preserved. Nos 32650 and 32670 are now at the heritage K&ESR while No 32662 is at Bressingham Gardens, Norfolk.

Services on the Hayling Island branch finished on 2 November 1963, when an intensive service was provided. Two train sets were in use, one running non-stop between Havant and the Island, and the other stopping at all stations. One of the latter, headed by Class 'A1X' 0-6-0 tank No 32650, is seen leaving North Hayling. No 32650 was built in December 1876 as LBSCR No 50 *Whitechapel*, and also spent time on the Isle of Wight as No W9 *Fishbourne*. It has also been preserved on the Kent & East Sussex Railway for many years. *Author*

Right: Class 'AIX' 0-6-0 tank No 32661 approaches Hayling Island station with a train from Havant during the summer of 1961. The engine was built in October 1875 as LBSCR No 61 *Sutton*. It was one of the few engines of its class that survived into 1963 not to be preserved.
M. E. J. Deane collection, courtesy of Ian Bennett

Below: When I travelled on the Hayling Island branch on a freezing-cold 12 January 1963, my train, the 2.20pm from Havant, was also hauled by Class 'AIX' No 32661. Before rejoining its train at Hayling Island for the return journey at 2.57pm the engine required more coal and has therefore stopped at the coaling stage where it was coaled by hand. *Both author*

Fratton shed (70F, later a sub-shed of 71A/70D): closed November 1959

My first visit to Fratton shed was on Easter Saturday 13 April 1963, as part of a 'shed bash' from Boscombe to Eastleigh and Brighton. Prior to the electrification of the lines into Portsmouth before the Second World War the shed had an allocation of more than 70 engines. As it had officially closed in 1959 I was not expecting to find much there. Nevertheless 'A1X' tank No 32670 from the Hayling Island branch was in steam in the extensive shed yard. I continued into the single turntabled roundhouse where I found most of the SR engines listed for preservation: 'Lord Nelson' Class 4-6-0 Lord Nelson, 'King Arthur' Class No 30777 Sir Lamiel, 'Schools' Class No 30945 Cheltenham, and 'M7' Class No 30245. A second 'Schools' Class there, No 30926 Repton, was waiting to be exported to the USA. The other engines present were Class 'N' and Class 'U' 'Moguls' Nos 31403 and 31808, Class 'Z' 0-8-0 tank No 30952 (withdrawn in November 1962), and Class 'Q1' 0-6-0s Nos 33026, 33031 and 33039.

My second visit was on 2 November while en route to Hayling Island. This time the 'Terrier' tank being serviced was No 32636 (built in 1872 as No 72 Fenchurch). It was sold to the Newhaven Harbour Co in 1898 but became Southern Railway No 636 in 1925. Like its shedmates it was withdrawn in November 1963 and is now preserved on the Bluebell Railway. The preserved engines had now been joined by Beattie 'well tank' No 30587. After later spending time at Buckfastleigh in Devon and at Wadebridge in Cornwall, it is now at the NRM's

'Locomotion' Museum at Shildon, County Durham. Class 'Z' No 30952 was also still there – was it being considered for preservation? If so it never happened! Other engines included Class 'Q' 0-6-0 No 30538, Class 'U' and 'Standard' Class 4 'Moguls' Nos 31803, 76006 and 76065, and three Class 'Q1s'.

The Isle of Wight

The railways of the Isle of Wight were the last to see the use of pre-Grouping engines and carriages on BR. It was also a place I associated with family day-trips by Roman City coach from Bath to Southampton. One of these was on Sunday 1 July 1962 when, after crossing to Cowes, we caught a train to Ryde (Esplanade) and back behind Class 'O2' 0-4-4 tank No 24 Calbourne. At the time 19 of these ex-LSWR tanks, built for the LSWR in the 1890s, were still active on the island. It was not until 16 October 1964 that I travelled on the island's second line, from Ryde (Pier) to Ventnor. The two lines split at Smallbook Junction west of Ryde (St John's). That day I caught the 8.48am from Bath Spa, arriving at Ryde (Pier) at 1.05pm. By coincidence, my train, the 1.25pm to Ventnor, was headed by Calbourne. As I waited for it to leave the station No 35 Freshwater arrived with the 1.11pm from Cowes. I returned on the 3.42pm, which was hauled by No 33 Bembridge. At Sandown we passed Calbourne again with the 3.25pm from Ryde (Pier) back to Ventnor. On returning to the mainland I caught the 5.45pm from Portsmouth & Southsea to Bath Spa, which was hauled as far as Salisbury by 'Standard' Class 4 No 76059.

My next visit was on Wednesday 25 August 1965 when I travelled to Southampton on my motor scooter to catch the ferry to Cowes. There I found a B&B for the night and caught the 2.24pm

as far as Ryde (St John's) behind No 29 Alverstone. At Havenstreet, then just a wayside station with a single central platform, we passed No 30 Shorwell on the 2.18pm from Ryde (Pier). I then travelled to Ventnor and back with No 28 Ashey before catching the 6.30pm from Ryde (Pier) to Cowes, again hauled by No 29 Alverstone. I alighted at the small station at Ashey where I photographed both Alverstone leaving and No 31 Chale approaching on the 6.24pm from Cowes. Finally I caught the 7.30pm from Ryde (Pier) back to my B&B and a fish & chip supper.

The lines from Smallbook Junction to Cowes and from Shanklin to Ventnor closed from 18 April 1966, but the Ryde (Pier) to Shanklin service was reprieved and electrified at the end of that year. Until then trains remained steam-hauled, so on Friday 27 May a friend and I travelled by scooter to Fareham and caught a train to Portsmouth (Harbour). At Ryde (Pier) we caught the 1.19pm to Shanklin headed by No 14 Fishbourne. As we waited for our train to leave, No 24 Calbourne arrived with the 12.55pm from Shanklin. On arrival at Shanklin No 14 ran round its train and returned us to Ryde (St John's) at 1.55pm where we visited the shed.

The steam service was finally withdrawn on Saturday 31 December 1966, although by then it only ran as far as Ryde (Esplanade) due to engineering work on the pier. The last day was marked by an LCGB railtour hauled by Nos 24 Calbourne and 31 Chale. Although a diesel shunter, No D2554 (Class 05), had arrived on the island for the electrification work, it had proved to be unreliable. The two 0-4-4 tanks were therefore retained and not withdrawn until March 1967. The new electric service started at the same time using redundant London Transport tube stock. Calbourne was subsequently preserved and is still active on the Isle of Wight Steam Railway.

Ryde shed (70H): closed December 1966

In 1930 the Southern Railway provided Ryde with a new two-road concrete and asbestos shed. By 1962 only Class 'O2' 0-4-4 tanks remained on the island, but until the end of 1960 the shed's allocation included four ex-LBSCR Class 'E1' 0-6-0 tanks; the last, No W4 *Wroxall* (ex-SR No 32694), was withdrawn that November. Several ex-LBSCR Class 'A1X' tanks were also based on the island for a time. In all, 23 Class 'O2' tanks went to the island, the first in 1923, the last two, Nos 35 *Freshwater* and 36 *Carisbrooke* (ex-SR Nos 30181 and 30198), in April 1949. I visited the depot on 28 August 1965 where I noted Nos 14 *Fishbourne*, 16 *Ventnor*, 17 *Seaview*, 20 *Shanklin*, 22 *Brading*, 26 *Whitwell* and 27 *Merstone*. All were withdrawn in January 1967 apart from No 26, which went in May 1966. See photo on page 74.

The Isle of Wight: Ryde (Pier) to Cowes

Class 'O2 0-4-4 tank No 24 *Calbourne* waits at Ryde (Pier) station with the 1.25pm to Ventnor on 16 October 1964. Approaching the station is sister engine No 35 *Freshwater* with the 12.31pm from Cowes. No 24 was among the last of its class to be withdrawn, in March 1967, after being used during the work to electrify the line to Shanklin. It was subsequently preserved and has been based on the Isle of Wight Steam Railway at Havenstreet ever since. *Freshwater* was withdrawn in October 1966. *Author*

Class 'O2' 0-4-4 tank No 28 *Ashey* approaches Ryde (Esplanade) with a train from Ryde (Pier) to Cowes in April 1963. The engine lasted until January 1967, when steam-operated services on the island ended. Note also the Ryde Pier tramway on the left. *M. E. J. Deane collection, courtesy of Ian Bennett*

Right: Class 'O2' 0-4-4 tank No 33 *Bembridge* arrives at Havenstreet, now the headquarters of the Isle of Wight Steam Railway, with a train to Cowes in April 1963. The engine was withdrawn in January 1967.
M. E. J. Deane collection, courtesy of Ian Bennett

Below: Class 'O2' 0-4-4 tank No 14 *Fishbourne* enters Cowes station with a train from Ryde (Pier) in April 1963. *Fishbourne* was also not withdrawn until January 1967. *M. E. J. Deane collection, courtesy of Ian Bennett*

Below right: Class 'O2' 0-4-4 tank No 29 *Alveston* stands in Cowes station with the 2.24pm to Ryde (Pier) on 25 August 1965. *Alveston* was withdrawn in May 1966. *Author*

Ryde (Pier) to Ventnor and Shanklin

Left: South of Ryde, the Cowes and Ventnor lines diverged at Smallbrook Junction. Here the fireman of Class 'O2' 0-4-4 tank No 28 *Ashey* surrenders the token for the single line from Brading; the train is the 5.20pm from Ventnor to Ryde (Pier) on 25 August 1965. The line was then double track through Ryde and onto the pier. *Author*

Below left: Class 'O2' 0-4-4 tanks Nos 29 *Alveston* and 35 *Freshwater* cross at Shanklin with trains to and from Ventnor in April 1963. *M. E. J. Deane collection, courtesy of Ian Bennett*

Below right: Class 'O2' 0-4-4 tank No 28 *Ashey* stands in Ventnor station with the 5.20pm to Ryde (Pier) on 25 August 1965. The mouth of the long tunnel between Ventnor and Wroxall is visible in the distance. The cost of maintaining this tunnel was part of the case for closing the line between Ventnor and Shanklin. *Author*

Left: The passenger service to Cowes was withdrawn from 21 February 1966, together with that between Shanklin and Ventnor. Steam-hauled trains from Ryde (Pier) then terminated at Shanklin until the end of the year, when the line was closed for electrification and still remains open today. Here at Shanklin 'O2' Class 0-4-4 tank No 14 *Fishbourne* has run round the 1.19pm from Ryde (Pier) and rejoins its train to form the 1.55pm return on 18 April 1966. Ten 'O2' tanks were retained to operate the service, which still involved two trains throughout the day. *Author*

Ryde shed (70H): closed December 1966

Below left: Two 'O2' Class 0-4-4 tanks stand outside Ryde shed on 5 September 1964. Nearest to the camera is No W35 *Freshwater*. The ex-LSWR 'O2' engines on the island were all built at Nine Elms between May 1890 and November 1892. *Frank Hornby*

Henstridge (S&D

Below right: In 1958 the WR took over the ex-S&D line from Bath (Green Park) to a point just north of Henstridge station. Here long-time resident of the line, 'Standard' Class 4 4-6-0 No 75072, arrives at Henstridge with a stopping train from Templecombe to Bournemouth (West) in November 1965. The engine was one of three allocated to Bath (Green Park) shed from new in 1956. It became a Templecombe engine in October 1962 and was withdrawn in December 1965.
M. E. J. Deane collection, courtesy of Ian Bennett

The last steam from Portsmouth, 1966-67

After visiting the Isle of Wight with a friend on 18 April 1966 we had travelled from Fareham to Havant on the 10.40am Plymouth to Brighton through train. At the time it was the only regular passenger train to use the line between Cosham and Farlington Junctions, and I wanted to travel on it. The train arrived at Fareham behind a Type 3 diesel-electric (later Class 33) and, after waiting 10 minutes to detach the Portsmouth coaches, it left around the tight left-hand curve towards Cosham. A Standard Class 4 2-6-0 was waiting to collect the Portsmouth & Southsea coaches on the line that ran straight on to Gosport's goods depot. The Plymouth to Brighton train had been diesel-hauled for some time but, when additional electrically heated coaches were needed on the SR's Central Division, steam-heated ones were substituted. As a result from November 1965 a Bulleid 'Light Pacific' was used between Brighton and Salisbury. This working was eliminated in the spring when steam-heating was no longer required. We had just missed it!

When my friend and I returned to Portsmouth (Harbour) after our trip to the Isle of Wight we found unrebuilt 'Battle of Britain' 'Pacific' No 34086 *219 Squadron* standing in the platform with a parcels train. Its single white disc on the right-hand side of the boiler indicated a train from Portsmouth to London Bridge via Horsham. Another parcels train also ran overnight from Portsmouth & Southsea to Waterloo via Eastleigh, where it combined with coaches from Weymouth. It remained steam-hauled until the end. The final SR steam-worked train from Portsmouth was a return excursion to Colne, Lancashire, on Sunday 9 July 1967. It ran via Guildford then through Kensington (Olympia) as far as Willesden Junction headed by rebuilt 'West Country' 'Pacific' No 34047, formerly *Callington*.

Part 5: HENSTRIDGE (S&D) to BROADSTONE and BOURNEMOUTH (West) including STALBRIDGE, STURMINSTER NEWTON and BLANDFORD FORUM

2P 4-4-0s built by the Midland Railway and the LMS were a feature of the ex-S&D line for more than 60 years; three were built at Derby in 1928 especially for the S&DJR. Their work ended after the summer of 1961 when they were withdrawn or put into store. In the spring of 1962 one of them, No 40563, was unexpectedly returned to service and is seen at Stalbridge during this period with a local to Bournemouth (West). The engine was withdrawn that May together with the last of the S&D engines, No 40634.
M. E. J. Deane collection, courtesy of Ian Bennett

Between 1958 and 1962 the former Somerset & Dorset (S&D) line was under WR control south of Templecombe to a point just north of Henstridge station. As described in Part 1, Templecombe station remained under SR control until the beginning of 1963, and the WR's boundary on the S&D was extended south to just north of Blandford Forum at the same time. Between 1958 and 1963 the motive power used on the line changed markedly. Despite the first appearance in 1958 of ex-GWR Class '2251' 0-6-0s and Class '57XX' pannier tanks, many trains were still hauled by 2P 4-4-0s and Class 3F and 4F 0-6-0s of either S&D, Midland or LMS origin.

The most modern engines were several Ivatt Class 2 2-6-2 tanks together with three 'Standard' Class 5 4-6-0s and three Class 4 4-6-0s, which went to Bath (Green Park) as new. More and more of these engines steadily replaced the older ones together with 'Standard' Class 3 2-6-2 and Class 4 2-6-4 tanks. Between 1960 and 1962 three 'Standard' Class 9F 2-10-0s were allocated to Bath (Green Park) to work the daily 'Pines Express' and Saturdays-only holiday trains out of Bath and over the Mendip Hills. Summer Saturdays also saw the use of the ex-S&D Class 7F 2-8-0s on passenger trains south of Templecombe. Bournemouth shed's 'West Country' 'Pacifics' were also regularly used on the trains. Unfortunately I never took any photos of S&D line trains south of Templecombe, so have had to fall back on those kindly provided by others. These go some way to illustrating the variety of engines used on the trains during the 1960s.

The ex-LMS/S&D 2P 4-4-0s were handsome engines and appeared regularly on passenger trains until the end of 1961. They were also used to double-head the heavier trains, including the 'Pines Express', over the Mendip Hills, being attached/detached at Evercreech Junction. Unexpectedly, one

'West Country' 'Pacific' No 34046 *Braunton*, with the northbound 'Pines Express', makes an unscheduled stop at Sturminster Newton to pass another train on Bank Holiday Monday, 6 August 1962. The latter is arriving behind 'Standard' Class 9F 2-10-0 No 92233 on the traditional Bank Holiday excursion from Bath (Green Park) to Bournemouth (West). Since 1960 four of these engines were sent to Bath to reduce the need for piloting on the summer trains. Towards the end of that summer the 9Fs included No 92220 *Evening Star*, which worked the last 'Pines Express' over the Mendips unaided on Saturday 8 September.
R. A. Lumber, courtesy of David Mitchell

of them, No 40563, was returned to steam early
in 1962; I photographed it leaving Bath with the
3.20pm from Green Park to Templecombe, while M.
E. J. Deane caught it at Stalbridge on a Templecombe
(as pictured in my 'Last BR Steam in Bath' book,
Recollections No. 64) to Bournemouth (West)
train during the same period. It was built in 1928 at
Derby for the LMS, the first of 135 new standard
engines. They were in fact virtually identical to many
older Midland Railway engines and were designed by
the same man, Sir Henry Fowler. Three more were
built specifically for the S&D in the same year, but
were absorbed into LMS stock in 1930 (BR Nos
40633 to 40635). No 40563 was among the last to
be withdrawn, in May 1962, together with ex-S&D
No 40634; both were Templecombe-based engines.

My recollections of the former Somerset
& Dorset line from Bath (Green Park) to
Templecombe are described in my 'Western Region'
book ('Railways & Recollections' No 110). As I say
there, several of my grandmother's sisters lived
around Bournemouth, so my journeys over the
line, including the southern half, were fairly regular.
I made two journeys to Bournemouth (West) on
the 'Pines Express' before it was diverted away
from the line. The first was at Easter 1962 when on
Thursday 19 April I travelled there with my aunt
and grandmother. At Bank Holiday times the 'Pines'
ran as two trains, from Manchester and Liverpool
respectively. We travelled on the latter train behind
rebuilt 'West Country' 'Pacific' No 34046 Braunton,
now preserved on the West Somerset Railway. My
last journey on the 'Pines' from Bath (Green Park)
was on Saturday 8 September 1962 when the train
was hauled unaided by 'Standard' Class 9F 2-10-0
No 92220 Evening Star on the train's last ever run.
With waving crowds all the way to Bournemouth,
I particularly remember people standing in their
back gardens next to the line as the train climbed

the bank from Poole to Branksome. It was a sad but
memorable journey!

My last journey on the southern half of the line
was on 6 March 1964 when I caught the 9.53am
from Green Park, hauled by 'Standard' Class 5 4-6-0
No 73049. As recounted in Part 2, I left the train at
Broadstone to travel to Brockenhurst, Lymington
(Pier) and Salisbury.

Above: Another familiar engine on the S&D line,
green-liveried 'Standard' Class 5 4-6-0 No 73054,
arrives at Sturminster Newton with the 5.30pm from
Bournemouth (West) to Templecombe during the
summer of 1963. This engine arrived at Bath (Green
Park) from Bristol (Barrow Road) shed in March
1961 and was withdrawn in August 1965.
M. E. J. Deane collection, courtesy of Ian Bennett

'Standard' Class 9F 2-10-0 No 92233 is seen again during the summer of 1962, standing in Blandford Forum station with a through train from the North to Bournemouth (West). At the end of the year the WR's influence over the S&D was extended from Henstridge to just north of Blandford Forum. In September 1962 No 92233 was reallocated to Ebbw Junction shed, Newport, but ended its days at Speke Junction, Liverpool, in February 1968.
M. E. J. Deane collection, courtesy of Ian Bennett

The specials of Saturday 1 and Sunday 2 January 1966

Over the years many special trains for enthusiasts travelled over the line. These came to a climax at the end of 1965 when the line was expected to close, and two railtours were organised on 1 and 2 January to 'celebrate' the line's closure. One was the LCGB's 'Mendip Merchantman' railtour, which left Waterloo behind 'Merchant Navy' 'Pacific' No 35011 *General Steam Navigation* on Saturday 1 January. Although the class was officially barred from the S&D line, the train ran to Templecombe via Bournemouth; it then ran to Highbridge behind two Ivatt tanks, leaving behind 9F 2-10-0 No 92243, which failed at Warmley near Bristol. The train eventually arrived back at Templecombe, where No 35011 returned the train to Waterloo via Salisbury . On the following day the RCTS's 'Somerset & Dorset' railtour again made use of *General Steam Navigation*. This time the 'Pacific' worked the train from Waterloo as far as Broadstone, where it was replaced by unrebuilt 'West Country' 'Pacific' No 34015 *Exmouth* and ex-SR Class 'U' 2-6-0 No 31639, which brought it into Bath. It then ran via Bristol to Highbridge and back to Templecombe. No 35011 again hauled the train back to Waterloo via Salisbury.

Because the necessary replacement bus services could not be implemented in time, the line was reprieved, but a temporary revised timetable was introduced. By then Bournemouth (West) had closed and S&D line trains used Bournemouth (Central) instead. Just five trains then left there for Templecombe each weekday, with a further train that started from Branksome at 1.25pm. Only one of these, the 6.45pm from Bournemouth (Central), ran through to Bath (Green Park), arriving there at 9.50pm. On Saturday 5 March this became the last service train ever to run into Green Park station,

'Standard' Class 4 No 75072 is seen again, this time arriving at Broadstone with the 4.44pm from Templecombe to Bournemouth (West) on 30 August 1961. The signals visible above the coaches apply to trains from Wimborne to Bournemouth. The S&D's line from Bath ended here and its trains then used the ex-LSWR/SR route to Bournemouth (West). *Terry Gough*

with me on board, and headed by 'Standard' Class 4 2-6-4s Nos 80043 and 80041.

The specials of Saturday 5 and Sunday 6 March 1966

Closure was finally fixed for Monday 7 March 1966, and two special trains ran on both Saturday 5 and Sunday 6 March. On the Saturday the GWR Society ran a special from Bath (Green Park) to Bournemouth (Central) and back behind 8F No 48706, while the LCGB organised a rerun of its January 'Somerset & Dorset' railtour. This left Waterloo for Templecombe via Salisbury behind the now preserved 'Merchant Navy' 'Pacific' No 35028 *Clan Line*. It then travelled to Highbridge and back to Evercreech Junction, from where it was taken over the Mendips to Bath by two unrebuilt 'Pacifics', 'West Country' No 34006 *Bude* and 'Battle of Britain' No 34057 *Biggin Hill*. The two engines later returned the railtour to Bournemouth, where No

35028 was waiting for the run back to Waterloo.

Next day, Sunday 6 March, 8F No 48706 and 'Standard' Class 4 2-6-4 tank No 80043 were waiting at Green Park to work the Stephenson Locomotive Society's 'Last passenger train from Bath to Templecombe and Bournemouth'. When this train returned to Bath it was the last passenger train ever to enter the terminus. The second special on the Sunday was the RCTS's 'Somerset & Dorset Farewell Railtour'. *Clan Line* again headed the train between Waterloo and Templecombe via Bournemouth (Central). The special then travelled to Highbridge where rebuilt 'West Country' 'Pacific' No 34013 *Okehampton* was waiting to haul it up the main line through Bristol (Temple Meads) to Mangotsfield. There 'Hymek' No D7014 replaced it for the run into Green Park. Meanwhile 'Battle of Britain' 'Pacific' No 34057 *Biggin Hill* had run light to Bath to work the special back to Templecombe. At Bath *Biggin Hill* was joined by *Okehampton*, which had turned on the triangle at Mangotsfield and run light to Green Park.

The two engines then became the last to haul a passenger train out of Green Park station over the S&D line to Templecombe, from where *Clan Line* returned the special to Waterloo via Salisbury.

The line from Broadstone to Blandford Forum stayed open for a time for military traffic. On Saturday 21 May 1966 it was visited by the 'Hampshire Explorer' railtour, organised by the British Young Travellers Society. This was hauled from Totton to Blandford Forum by 'Standard' Class 3 2-6-0 No 77014, the only member of its class to be shedded on the SR. It later hauled the train back to Broadstone, from where unrebuilt 'West Country' 'Pacific' No 34006 *Bude* took it to Ringwood, then returned it to Bournemouth (Central) (see the photograph on page 46).

Below: 'Standard' Class 4 2-6-0 No 76015 leaves Bournemouth (West) with the 1.00pm to Bath (Green Park). The Class 4 2-6-4 tank seen in the background has arrived on an earlier S&D line train and will later work back to Templecombe or Bath. After Bournemouth (West) closed in September 1965 these trains used Bournemouth (Central) station. *Ray Ruffell, Slip Coach Archive*

The last Saturday: 5 March 1966

Above: Two railtours were organised on Saturday 5 March 1966 to 'celebrate' the S&D's final closure. One of them was a GWR Society special that ran from Bath (Green Park) to Bournemouth (Central) and back behind 8F 2-8-0 No 48706. These views of the signal boxes at Henstridge (the first picture) and Blandford Forum were taken from the train. Next day No 48706 and 'Standard' Class 4 2-6-4 tank No 80043 worked the Stephenson Locomotive Society's 'Last passenger train from Bath to Templecombe and Bournemouth'. When the special returned to Bath (Green Park) it was the last passenger train ever to enter the terminus. Both engines were withdrawn the following day. *Author's collection*